SPECTACULAR BOND

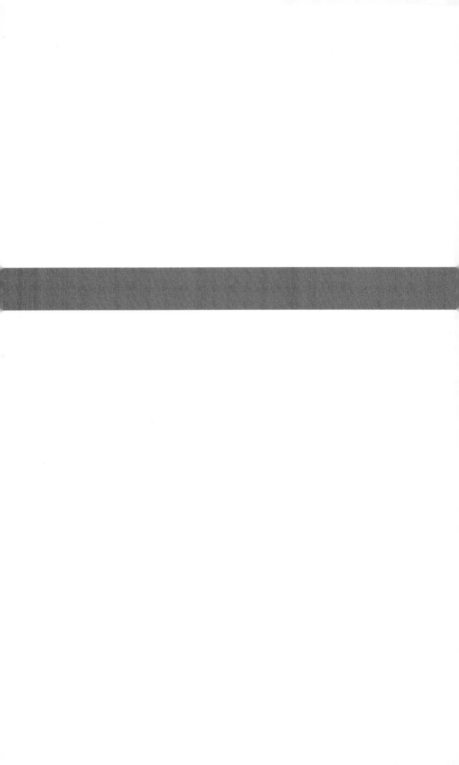

SPECTACULAR BOND

Reaching the Child with Autism

by

Marion Blank, Ph.D.
Suzanne Goh, M.D.
and
Susan Deland

Cover design by Wendy Bass Design

Book design by Jamie Kerry of Belle Étoile Studios
www.belleetoilestudios.com

First edition.

Library of Congress Control Number: 2013910660

ISBN 978-0-9895462-0-1

Printed and bound in the United States of America

This work has come to fruition through the assistance of many families, colleagues, and institutions, and we would like to express our deep appreciation to them.

The families we have worked with are amazing in their dedication and commitment, and they have been generous in opening their hearts, minds and homes to us. We would particularly like to express our appreciation to Kathy Broad and Pete Booth, Arlene and Mitchel Maidman, Burt and Lynn Manning, Eloisa and Alain Principe, Clara and Brian Rogers, Christina and Kent Turner, and, of course, Alex Deland and Alex Deland, Jr.

Among our colleagues at Columbia University, special thanks go to Dr. Jeffrey Lieberman, Dr. Bradley S. Peterson, Dr. Agnes Whitaker, Dr. Andrew Gerber, and Dr. Molly Algermissen. In the "wider world," we are grateful for the support and guidance of Lindsey Alexander, Wendy Bass, Paola Bellu, Jonathan Blank, Alisa Dror, Michelle and Jeff Hasson, Neil Hattangadi, Michael Hinesly, Portia Iverson, Jamie Kerry, Davida Kugelmass, Jacqui Leboutillier, Lan Li, Karen Quinn, Cathy Schaeffer, Joanne Tombrakos, and Penni Urquhart.

We also want to thank Autism Speaks and the American Brain Foundation for their support of the research on the program; Paul and Daisy Soros Fellowships for New Americans for their generous support of Dr. Goh's medical career; JP Morgan Private Bank for providing the family-friendly environment that was so vital to Susan when her daughter Diane was first diagnosed; Pelham community and Pelham Union Free School District for all they have done to support the Deland family; and the Texas Autism Conference and its coordinator, Laura Cantu, for helping to spread the ideas and methodology to teachers and practitioners.

We dedicate this book to our families and to all the families of children with autism we've been blessed to know.

Contents

Part 3: Entering the Wider World

Preface

The world of autism is a whirlwind of contradictions. On the one hand, there are unique stories of individuals who display amazing, genius-level skills in areas such as math, science, engineering, or music. On the other hand, studies find that many, if not most, of the children in this growing epidemic fail to achieve significant language and require supervision throughout adult life. Amazingly, both positions are valid. At the same time, they are incomplete. Each represents a narrow slice of the vast continuum that is autism.

In our experience tremendous results are attainable for the great majority of children. The kind of effort required, however, is different from what is offered in mainstream treatment models. It is based on a relationship that has been the foundation of human existence from time immemorial—the *parent-child bond*.

In the many controversies that have marked the field, this basic notion was abandoned. This seems due, in large part, to the work of psychiatrist Dr. Bruno Bettleheim who wrote the book *The Empty Fortress: Infantile Autism and the Birth of the Self* in 1967. In it he attempted to use his knowledge of war survivors to "explain" autism. His experience showed him that extreme environments could produce autistic-like behaviors. He thought a similar process had to be at work in children with autism, and he placed the responsibility on parents. The grievous damage done by this cannot be overstated.

Another tragic but unrecognized outcome has been to close off any consideration of the parent-child relationship and its crucial role in transforming the child's future. We have found that parents of children with autism have a degree of commitment and devotion that is extraordinary. Because of the unique nature of autism, however, key components of the relationship do not emerge in the automatic way that marks typical development. The challenges that the children face with social reciprocity and communication close them off from much of what their parents have to offer.

The children can be reached, and they can blossom, but only through conscious care and attention to reshaping patterns of parent-child interaction that normally function outside of awareness. *The parent is not the cause of the syndrome, but the parent-child bond holds the key to any successful outcome.*

Not only is the transformed bond an essential ingredient in empowering the children, it is also critical to the effectiveness of other therapies. It serves as the foundation on which successful intervention in language, communication, and social interaction are built. When it is in place, the achievements are astonishing; when it is not, other efforts flounder. Why this is the case and how to create a *spectacular bond* with your own child is the message of this book.

About the Authors

This book is a collaboration that integrates three points of view: one from a psychologist—Marion Blank, one from a neurologist—Suzanne Goh,and one from a parent—Susan Deland. This partnership allows us to bring together, in a single book,

- the neurological and psychological foundations of autism

- a scientific rationale for why and how the behaviors can be changed

- a family's successful experience in creating a spectacular bond, and

- a step-by-step guide for how you can do this with your own child.

Marion Blank, Ph.D., is a developmental psychologist as well as an internationally recognized pioneer in the field of language education for children with learning disabilities. She is a member of the faculty of the Department of Psychiatry at Columbia University and is former Professor in the Department of Psychiatry at Rutgers Medical School. She is the author of *The Reading Remedy: Six Essential Skills That Will Turn Your Child into a Reader* and has published over 60 articles and book chapters on language disabilities. She is the designer of the widely used language software programs *The Sentence Master* and *Reading Kingdom* and one of the creators of the *Preschool Learning Assessment Instrument*, a leading neuropsychological test for the diagnosis of learning disabilities in young children. She has been associated as editor and author with numerous journals and publications, including *Child Development, Journal of Applied Psycholinguistics*, and *Topics in Learning and Language Disabilities*.

* * *

My first encounters with autism took place in England when I was a graduate student. At the time, autism was an extremely rare condition that received little attention from the world of psychology. Standing in marked contrast to the general neglect were two psychologists in London—Beate Hermelin and Neil O'Connor—who were carrying out fascinating research aimed at trying to uncover the secrets of this enigmatic condition. I followed their research closely, but for the most part, I was an outsider looking in.

My involvement changed dramatically some years later. By that time, the number of cases of autism was expanding rapidly. I was well known for my work in developing language intervention programs, and parents and schools began to consult me about how my work might be adapted to aid children on the spectrum. I was excited to move in that direction, and I began working intensively with the children.

Fortunately, the effort paid off, and the programs I developed yielded positive results.

Still, I was not totally comfortable with what was taking place. One major source of the unease stemmed from the difficulties the children displayed with the introduction of new material. They seemed to possess super-sensitive antennas so that even slight changes in activity were met with a range of negative behaviors that included meltdowns, tuning out, increased stimming, a seeming loss of skills and on and on.

When I raised my concerns with colleagues, the typical response was, "Of course, children with autism have great difficulties with transitions." The prevailing belief was that behavioral problems like the ones I described were part and parcel of the condition, and essentially nothing could be done about them.

The response seemed so strange. On the one hand, without a shred of doubt, intensive efforts were being put forth to alter the children's language and cognition; on the other hand, also without a shred of doubt, behavioral issues were considered intractable and a factor that one had to accept and live with. The contradiction was amazing. Even more significantly, I began to wonder if perhaps it was "wrong."

This book details the journey that I embarked on once I began to follow my doubts. The end result has been phenomenally rewarding. Although the work is challenging and demanding, I found that my skepticism was well founded. Behavioral issues that plague the lives of children on the autism spectrum can be overcome. Step by step, my ideas evolved into a program called the Behavioral Organization Needed for Development (BOND). That acronym was fitting because, as the work progressed, it was clear that the parent-child bond was critical to success. So BOND became the Spectacular Bond that you are going to read about here. It has been extraordinarily gratifying to see the peace, security and happiness that it brings to children and their families.

Suzanne Goh, M.D., is a pediatric neurologist and neuroscience researcher. She has served as Associate Research Scientist and Assistant Professor of Clinical Neurology in the Division of Child Psychiatry at Columbia University. She is former Co-Director of the Columbia University Developmental Neuropsychiatry Program for Autism and Related Disorders. Her research focuses on metabolic disturbances in autism and on the use of brain imaging to identify differences in brain circuits in autism. A Rhodes Scholar, she graduated from Harvard University, University of Oxford, and Harvard Medical School. She has published research articles in numerous journals, including *Neurology, Annals of Neurology, Pediatric Neurology, Developmental Cognitive Neuroscience,* and *Developmental Medicine & Child Neurology.*

* * *

My passion for what I do comes from the children that I work with and their amazing families. They inspire me every day. When I first started working in autism clinics as a student, I was frustrated by what I saw. Children usually came in just once a year for an evaluation. They left with lengthy reports that were hard to decipher and had a set of standard recommendations. The focus was on establishing a diagnosis, but parents often left without a clear plan for what needed to be done. I didn't see how this sort of setup could accomplish meaningful change.

Then I met Marion Blank in 2008 when I joined Columbia University. She allowed me to observe her sessions with patients, and I was immediately inspired. Nothing else I had encountered in the field of autism treatment fit so well with what I knew about the neuroscience of the developing brain. I felt strongly that parents in search of the best treatment should know about her work. I told Marion this, and a few weeks later this book started taking shape.

As we began to detail the program, we realized that the story was incomplete without the perspective of the families, for they were the ones who made it all happen. That led us to invite Susan Deland to be a co-author. She could describe what it was like on a day-to-day basis to implement the program. To our delight, she agreed and that was how our unique parent-professional partnership came about.

Susan Deland is the mother of 13-year-old Diane and 14-year-old Alex. She is a Certified Public Accountant and has had a career in finance in New York City. Diane was diagnosed with an Autism Spectrum Disorder (ASD) at the age of three. After that diagnosis, Susan's primary focus was on finding and implementing the interventions that would give Diane the best chance at a rewarding future. This led her to Dr. Blank and the Spectacular Bond program. That decision, in turn, has led her on a journey that she describes as "exceeding all of the dreams" she had for Diane and the whole family.

* * *

I am honored to have been asked by Dr. Blank and Dr. Goh to provide the parent voice in this book. Diane is one of the many children who have had their lives transformed by Dr. Blank's techniques. When Diane was first diagnosed with ASD, I received many pessimistic warnings from professionals. But discussions with other families convinced me that this was not the full story. I believed that with the right environment, Diane had the potential for a bright and independent future. Dr. Blank wholeheartedly shared that belief—not only did she believe as strongly as I did in Diane's future, she had a concrete plan of action for getting Diane there.

Each step of the way, the program was set up to help Diane master a set of skills and to move consistently to higher and higher levels of functioning. At the same time we felt it was equally important to maintain a healthy family balance. The Spectacular Bond program recognizes the need to work with the realities of family life so that all members of the family can flourish. It also recognizes the unique qualities of children on the spectrum and gives them the foundation they need so that their individual personalities can shine through. In this time of highly segmented and specialized services, Spectacular Bond offers a different kind of approach—a holistic, parent-centered intervention.

It also produces powerful results that ultimately enhance the effectiveness of any other interventions that are offered.

Throughout this book, you will read about my family's journey and you will see how this program has made all the difference for our Diane. You will also gain access to the insights, advice, and at-home methods that will enable you to bond with your child in a new way that promotes all aspects of development. If I can help other families achieve what we have and what we know is possible, I will be deeply gratified.

Introduction

Is this book right for me?

This book outlines "the what, the why, and the how" of the Spectacular Bond program. It is designed primarily for children on the autism spectrum who are between two to six years of age, and in some cases, may be used with children up to ten years of age. Older children can also benefit from many of the techniques in this program, but direct professional guidance is usually needed.

The program is grounded in an interdisciplinary approach that uses the latest advances in key scientific disciplines including linguistics, neuroscience, and the psychology of parent-child interactions. It is designed to bring about significant changes in short periods of time. Improvements in the children's behaviors are often evident within two to four weeks. When the method is implemented with precision, entirely new patterns of behavior can be in place within three months.

To implement the program, you will need to alter many aspects of the way you live your life—from how you speak to your child, to the way you go about daily routines, and even the way you show your child affection. Modifications of this nature are extraordinarily challenging. You need to become comfortable with being uncomfortable. As one parent put it,

"*The program went against almost everything I believed I should be doing, but I took it on. Once I saw the changes that were possible, I had to offer that opportunity to my child.*" Some of those changes can be seen in the videos available at www.spectacularbond. com.

By now, your mind is likely to be stirring with a host of thoughts and emotions. If one of them is, "I will move heaven and earth to offer my child these opportunities," then read on!

PART 1

Setting the Stage for Change

1

An Enlightening and Inspirational Visit

The noblest pleasure is the joy of understanding.

— Leonardo Da Vinci

This book is a joint effort of three authors—a psychologist, a neurologist, and me—a mom of a child with autism. My search to help our daughter, Diane, led me to the Spectacular Bond program nearly ten years ago.

When we started the program, Diane could not communicate in any meaningful way. She was almost entirely lost in her own world. Today, she is a vibrant thirteen-year-old, participating in several mainstream seventh grade classes. She enjoys reading and writing and has an array of interests, hobbies, and meaningful friendships.

The program has allowed me to understand how Diane sees and experiences the world. There is great satisfaction in understanding something that has been puzzling, and few things are as puzzling as a child with autism. Understanding means not simply knowing, but knowing *what to do*. It means taking actions to change things and being confident that those actions fit with the way my daughter's brain works and with her view of the world.

I am not the only one to want the pleasure and power of understanding. I believe that Diane and all children with autism spectrum disorders (ASD) are also capable and deserving of that experience. The Spectacular Bond program brings this dream to reality.

The best way to give you a sense of the journey that my family and I have been on is to start where it all began—in an office at Columbia University. I can think of no other two-hour period in my life that so dramatically altered my thinking. It was as if a bolt of lightning struck and permanently changed the course of our lives.

* * *

It was a spring day in New York City in the month of April 2003. Two weeks earlier, our three-year-old daughter Diane had been diagnosed with autism.

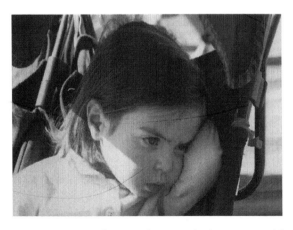

The neurologist who first made Diane's diagnosis told us in no uncertain terms that there was no cure. He warned us to avoid the trap that many parents in our situation fall into by becoming consumed with fruitless efforts to help their child. He said that Diane was cute and that this would make other people more tolerant of her disability.

In one breath, we were given a devastating diagnosis, and in the next, we were told to accept that there was no meaningful treatment. Of course, we rejected his warning and immediately immersed ourselves in the literature on autism and its different therapies. We talked to other parents, met with therapists, and made trips to schools and training centers for children with autism. It was this search that led us on that spring day to the office of Dr. Marion Blank.

Dr. Blank came to the waiting area to greet us. She was a petite older woman with short strawberry-blond curls. We all walked into her office and sat down. Diane followed us in and ran around the room on her toes, chirping and flapping.

"Diane, please come over here and sit next to Mommy," I said. Diane continued running around the room, ignoring my request. "Diane," my husband Alex tried, "Come over here!" Dr. Blank held up her hand to stop him.

"Don't try to get her to sit right now," said Dr. Blank. "As you see, she's going to ignore you. Every time you ask her to do something and she doesn't do it, you're sending the message that you're powerless over her and that you have no control over what she does. That is *not* a good message. The room is childproof, and it's safe for her to wander around. So sit back and don't worry right now about getting her to do anything."

I looked at Dr. Blank, trying to process her words, when I heard Alex say, "Look Diane, isn't this a nice toy?" Diane ignored him, almost as if to prove the point that Dr. Blank had just made.

I turned to Dr. Blank, "Do you mean that Diane can do what we ask, but she chooses not to?"

Dr. Blank said, "Well, let's think about it this way. Is Diane capable of sitting in a chair? Yes, of course. She sits in a chair all the time, but only when she wants to, not when you ask her to. Is Diane capable of looking at a toy? Of course. I'm sure you make dozens of requests every day for things that you know she can do. You wouldn't ask her to do something she can't. The question is why she does things when she wants to but not when you ask her to."

We had no idea why Diane would not do simple things that we asked her to do, even when we had seen her do those things on her own. We assumed that it was part of having autism, but no one had ever offered us a deeper explanation.

Dr. Blank explained that children with ASD tune out from the world and particularly from people because they find the world around them to be noxious. She explained that children with ASD process incoming information very differently than other children. For example, although most children love to hear the human voice, children with ASD find voices to be hard to interpret, constantly changing, and unpredictable. The same is true for processing visual information (such as faces) and motor information (such as gestures). Children with ASD are drawn to inanimate objects because they are simple and easier to control. People, by contrast, are complex and present a constant flood of changing sensory input.

Children with ASD tune out much of the world because the rush of sensory stimulation can be overwhelming and even painful.

Dr. Blank offered an analogy that I'll never forget. She said that for children with ASD, life in the world of people can be like living in a washing machine. The onslaught of unpredictable stimulation feels overwhelming and unending. It makes sense that they would prefer to spend their time lining up objects or flipping switches on and off. The only chance for some semblance of tranquility is to tune out the world.

I said to Dr. Blank, "I don't want to let her tune us out. Should we try to stop her from doing that?"

"Well, there are some who think that we should let the children remain isolated in their own worlds," she said. "They believe that we should not intervene in any way to alter the child's unique qualities. This belief is tempting in some ways, but it rests on the assumption that young children already possess the wisdom to make the right decisions about what they learn and what they do. A consequence of that approach is that children aren't given the skills they need to understand and learn from others."

What Dr. Blank was saying was something that Alex and I already believed—that all children need the guidance of adults. Without that guidance, they cannot learn the skills they need to become independent. More than anything, we wanted Diane to be happier. Even the simplest demands from us could lead to outbursts and meltdowns. We did not want her to experience the world as such a tumultuous and dangerous place.

"The key," said Dr. Blank, "is to strike the right balance where we get Diane to tune in to us so that we can teach her the social behaviors, language, and cognitive skills that she needs in order to develop and grow. At the same time, we can't overwhelm her with input that will cause her to retreat even further from us."

> The key to success is to get the children tuned in so they can learn important skills but not to overwhelm them with input that will cause them to retreat further from us.

"How does this fit in with her temper tantrums?" I asked. "She seems to go back and forth between tuning out and having tantrums."

"Hard as it may be to believe," said Dr. Blank, "the tantrums are simply the other side of the coin."

The reason that Diane had frequent meltdowns, explained Dr. Blank, was because she couldn't completely block us out. There were many times throughout each day that we insisted on inserting ourselves into her world. We might try to get her to sit for mealtime or force her to take a bath or brush her teeth. These were the times when she would switch gears—from tuning us out to fighting us.

Doing this was her way of protecting herself. It was her way of making sure that almost nothing from the world of people intruded into the simpler world she was striving to create. She did accept a few familiar activities that were pleasurable in some way, like being twirled around or bounced, but beyond that she was determined to keep us from intruding and from controlling her behavior.

Alex said, "Many people—both parents and professionals— have told us that Diane's out-of-control behavior is part of what autism is and that we can't expect things to be any other way. But you are saying that Diane is capable of controlling herself. Right now we're spending so much energy trying to find ways to avoid triggering a tantrum, but it's not working. We know she would be happier if she could hold herself together. We just hadn't thought it was possible."

"The first step is for you to realize that it *is* possible," said Dr. Blank. "The next step is for you to make changes in your own behavior so that Diane faces a different, far less confusing and less dangerous world. We can't ask her to come out of her own world unless we provide her with a safe alternative."

We can't expect children with ASD to come out of their world into ours unless we provide a safe alternative.

"How do we do that?" asked Alex.

"The basic principle is not complicated," said Dr. Blank. "We are going to make *her* world much simpler. We do this by putting in place a set of clear rules for you to follow. For example, one rule is to stop asking her all questions. Questions are the hardest form of language for a child with autism to understand. Simple statements and commands are much easier. For example, what are some questions that you've asked her today?"

Alex replied, "Can you say hi to Daddy? Can you get in the car now?"

Dr. Blank said, "Did she do what you asked?"

Alex and I both answered, "No."

"You were giving her commands in the form of a question, which is very confusing for children who have difficulties with communication. On top of that, when you ask questions that she doesn't respond to, she gets the message that you are someone who is hard to understand *and* someone who is powerless."

"I never thought of it that way," I said. "We're actually pressuring her in ways that make her life harder and that make her want to tune us out more. Everyone else has told us that she needs language stimulation and questions are the best way to get it."

"That's the common advice, but take it with caution," said Dr. Blank. "Do you know the term that lawyers use for asking someone questions repeatedly? Interrogation. Think of the stress and anxiety that come with being interrogated. In the beginning we simply don't want to add to the stress she's facing when it's not necessary. Eliminating questions, just on its own, is an important step."

This seemed unusual, but Dr. Blank explained to us that it was only temporary. Simplifying our language would allow Diane to feel more comfortable. Once she could handle simple forms of language, we would gradually build in greater complexity. "Piling on complex language in the beginning," said Dr. Blank, "is like taking a toddler who has just learned to walk and asking her to run a marathon."

Simplifying the child's environment and reducing complex language is a critical first step.

Alex and I looked at each other. No one had ever explained it to us like this before, and it was so powerfully logical. "What is it exactly that we'll have to do?" I asked. "I still don't think we really understand what the whole program involves."

To give us a better sense of what the program involved and, even more importantly, what it could accomplish, Dr.

Blank showed us some before-and-after videos of children at the outset of the program and then several months later. The changes were amazing. Children who initially had been screaming like Diane were sitting attentively in teaching sessions, effectively using language, and obviously enjoying the mastery of new skills. All this was taking place without a single reward—no M&Ms, no bubbles, no favorite toys.

We were stunned. "How do you get the children to do all that?"

"There are too many steps to explain all at once," said Dr. Blank, "but you can get a sense of what they involve by seeing one of the first activities you'll do with Diane called '*quiet sitting.*' It's a simple but powerful technique. We are going to ask her to do something that we know she easily can do—after all, she sits quietly when she's watching TV or eating a snack. The difference now is that she will be doing it *at your request.* That will be a first step in getting her to see that you have the right and the ability to control her behavior. To show you how it's done, I'm going to have Diane sit here next to me."

"All right," I said, "but you realize that she probably won't do it, don't you?"

"Yes, I would be shocked if she did. What I'm going to do is set things up so that she must sit. That means holding her and keeping her here even if she starts to pull away. Of course, if you don't want me to do that, just say so and I'll stop at any time."

Dr. Blank brought Diane next to her, sat her down on the floor, and kept her from getting up by holding her firmly at the shoulders. Right away, Diane started screaming.

Alex and I stared in disbelief as Dr. Blank did nothing to stop Diane's screaming. She did not try to distract her or comfort her. At the same time, she would not allow Diane to get up. Diane's crying was unnerving to us as it always was, but we were reassured by Dr. Blank's calm manner. No other professional we had met seemed so at ease with Diane.

After about two minutes, Diane stopped screaming and stayed seated with an unhappy look on her face. We continued our discussion while she sat there.

"Maybe it's too soon to ask this," said Alex, "but if we decide to do the program with you, what will we be working toward? What can we hope for?"

Dr. Blank said, "I wish I could give a definite answer, but it depends on so many factors. It depends on how well I guide you, it depends on how well you implement the guidelines, and it depends on Diane's unique biology. Embedded in what I just said is a key principle. At all points, the work is a partnership. It is not just a matter of the child changing."

Dr. Blank then pointed out several things that indicated Diane could make great strides. One was that Diane already had some spoken language. It meant that despite being overwhelmed by the chaos in the world around her, she had been able to extract some language. Another good sign was the fact that her self-stimulatory behaviors tended to last for only a few minutes at a time, rather than for hours.

"Can I promise success?" said Dr. Blank. "No. Do we have a good chance of success? Yes."

"What do you mean by success?" I asked.

"For Diane to be open and receptive to learning from you and from her teachers with little resistance," said Dr. Blank. "Once she is open and willing to learn from others, she can begin to develop an enormous range of skills. She can learn to communicate meaningfully with others. She can develop relationships with family and friends that involve the real sharing of thoughts and emotions. Can I guarantee that she will go to college and get married one day? No, but no one can guarantee that for even a typically developing child. Our goal is to put in place the building blocks that will allow for that sort of success in the future."

In the Spectacular Bond program success means creating the foundation for communication, meaningful relationships, and learning.

At this point, Diane continued to sit calmly next to Dr. Blank without being held or restrained in any way. I had no recollection of ever seeing her this calm for this extended a time. All this in one session! Now I could see how rapid change might be possible.

Dr. Blank looked at Diane and said, "You can get up now, Diane." Diane jumped up, ran over to us, and squeezed herself between Alex and me on the sofa. We had not seen her do something like this in months. We were thrilled. We showed our delight by smothering her with hugs and kisses. "Great job, Diane! You did such a good job! Mommy and Daddy are so proud of you!"

Dr. Blank immediately interrupted us. "I know this is going to be hard for you to hear, but you must stop giving this level of praise and affection. You should simply smile and say, 'That was good, Diane.'"

"Why not more?" I asked.

"It's great that you are pleased, and you should be, but you have to remember that part of having autism means that Diane has very little motivation to do things that please other people. It's a mistake for you to think that the more pleasure you show, the more likely she is to repeat this good behavior the next time."

Dr. Blank also explained that our effusive response presented her with gestures, emotions, and vocalizations that were confusing and possibly overwhelming to her. They also created a distorted social environment. "It's as if I asked you to close the door, and, after you did it, I started applauding and saying what a fabulous job you've done," said Dr. Blank. "Calm, effective social interaction is what we are seeking and what the child should begin to expect."

"Even more important," she said, "is that you need to start sending her a new message. That message from here forward is that you are going to make some clear, simple requests of her, and you have the power to ensure that they will be done."

"I'm starting to get a sense for why this will be difficult," I said. "As it is, we have little affection and interaction from her. What if that goes away completely? I'm afraid that if I become more demanding, she'll turn away from me even more. After everything we've been through, I don't think we could take that."

"I understand," said Dr. Blank. "That is the biggest concern I hear, but I assure you that Diane's bond to you is very strong. It will become even stronger through this program. The program is specifically designed to create a much stronger, more effective, and more rewarding relationship. The changes also come quickly, so in a few weeks you'll see exactly what I mean."

Alex said, "It sounds like the work will really rest on us. Is there room for other people to help?"

"You are the most important people in her life, and what you do with her sets the framework for everything else. But you do not have to do it all on your own," said Dr. Blank. "Tutors, nannies, baby sitters, or family members can all be a great help. But your involvement is key. If she senses that you are not on board, the program won't work. Keep in mind, too, that the time needed to implement the program is not as much as you might imagine. Over the course of the day, Diane will be meaningfully engaged with you for about one to two hours per day and no more. One of the most important things for you to know is that *more is not always better*. Doing the right things, in the right amounts, at the right times will be the key to success."

* * *

If one word could capture the feeling we had when we left Dr. Blank's office that day, it is *enlightened*. We saw ourselves and Diane in a totally new light. Anyone who has ever experienced an "AHA!" moment will know something about what we felt. In a flash we were made aware of a reality that we had never seen before, and it made such perfect sense. We felt incredibly hopeful. We had found a guide to help us create a bridge between our world and Diane's.

Diane Deland at age 5

 To see videos of Diane Deland, visit www.spectacularbond.com.

Key factors in our decision to begin the Spectacular Bond program

Clear markers: The changes in the single session were astonishing. If our efforts resulted in change at all like that, it would transform our lives.

Fast results: We would know within a few months if the program was working.

Effects on other therapies: The program would make Diane more receptive to learning—not just from us, but from other adults, too, which meant that other therapies we were planning for her would be more effective.

A consistent and comprehensible world: Through the program we would learn to understand Diane's world and the source of her difficulties, and she would begin to understand our world. The world of therapy and the world of family would also be unified. Diane was not going to receive one set of messages from her therapists and another set at home.

Family dynamics: The limited time required by the program would free us up to be with our son, who also needed our attention.

Hope restored: Goals that we had thought would no longer be possible for Diane seemed possible again. The videos of children who had completed the program were unbelievably powerful. (Later we talked with other parents and met their children—they were truly engaged in the world in a way that we had not seen elsewhere). Language, reading, social relationships, and a full, independent life were all now a part of Diane's future.

2

The World Through
the Child's Eyes

As a child I remember Mother asking me time and again, "Temple, are you listening to me? Look at me." Sometimes, I wanted to, but couldn't.

— Temple Grandin, *Emergence: Labeled Autistic*

The nuts and bolts of the program are outlined in detail in Part 2 of the book, and if you have the urge to get started right away, you can look ahead. But we encourage you to take a few days to read and reflect on the chapters here in Part 1. They cover the fundamentals on which the program rests. An understanding of those fundamentals makes you better equipped to successfully carry out the program.

The creation of a partnership—a working relationship between the child and the parent—is one of those fundamentals. To achieve this, we need to understand the perspective of each member of the partnership.

We begin here by trying to see the world through the child's eyes. That is no easy feat. After all, many children with ASD cannot tell us what they are thinking or feeling. Fortunately, a growing number of individuals with ASD have written about their experiences, and we can learn a tremendous amount from what they have to say.

Some Firsthand Accounts

Two important themes raised by authors with ASD are particularly relevant to the child's daily life. One is hypersensitivity to stimulation, and the other is methods of coping with that hypersensitivity.

> "From as far back as I can remember, I always hated to be hugged.... It was just too overwhelming. It was like a great, all-engulfing tidal wave of stimulation, and I reacted like a wild animal." (T. Grandin, *Thinking in Pictures*)

> "My hearing is like having a hearing aid with the volume control stuck on 'super loud.' It is like an open microphone that picks up everything. I have two choices: turn the mike on and get deluged with sound, or shut it off." (T. Grandin, "An Inside View of Autism")

> "Smells like deodorant and aftercare lotion, they smell so strong to me I can't stand it, and perfume drives me nuts." (A. Stehli, *The Sound of a Miracle*)

> "I felt that all touching was pain, and I was frightened." (D. Williams, *Nobody Nowhere*)

To cope with these sensitivities, children adopt behaviors that help them tune out from the world around them.

"Grinding my teeth kept disturbing, unpredictable, and meaningless outside noise from coming in. Singing a repetitive tune and humming continuously did the same. The tapping gave a continuous rhythm and stopped the unpatterned movement of others from invading." (D. Williams, *Somebody Somewhere*)

"...when I was in the world of people, I was extremely sensitive to noises..." "[By fixating on spinning objects] I saw nothing or heard nothing...no sound intruded on my fixation. It was as if I were deaf. Even a sudden loud noise didn't startle me from my world." (T. Grandin, *Emergence: Labeled Autistic*)

An Intense World

As these examples demonstrate, individuals with autism find much of the outside world to be unpleasant. Ordinary, everyday sounds and sensations can be overwhelming, painful, and even frightening. This leads many children to develop patterns of avoidance.

Henry and Kamila Markram, two leading neuroscientists, have formulated the "intense world" theory to explain sensory discomfort in autism. They believe that the children experience overactivity in the brain networks that process sensory information. The resulting brain activity leads the children to experience what we think of as "ordinary" sounds, sights, textures, tastes, and smells to be painfully intense and something to be avoided. It's somewhat like being in a theater where the sound equipment goes awry and the screeching sounds can be unbearable. Understandably, the children withdraw from the world.

Diane's Hypersensitivities

From the time she was two years old, Diane hated the sound of vacuum cleaners and hairdryers. She could not be in the house if the vacuum was running. She stood outside the front door, waiting to see that the vacuum cleaner had been returned to the closet, before coming back in. We could not use hairdryers anywhere in the home, even behind closed doors.

She was especially sensitive to the sound of crying infants, and that made it hard for us to go out in public. At a restaurant she could hear the arrival of a whimpering child well before the child could be seen. I remember her saying, "Go home, baby." I would look around, see no baby in sight, and I would say, "Diane, there are no babies here." Moments later I would see that, indeed, a small child had arrived. If there was more than a slight noise from the child, Diane panicked. One time she lunged at a baby, and I feared she would attack him to stop the noise."

The problem extends beyond intensity from a single modality, such as hearing or vision. The world is not neatly packaged so that one input comes in at a time. Instead, most situations have multiple inputs that include voices, faces, background noise, and tactile sensations. Research indicates that children with ASD have even greater difficulty when input is coming in from multiple senses at once.

Hypersensitivities Can Change Over Time

Development is a powerful, ongoing process, and sensitivities often do diminish as children mature. By the time children are older, however, they may have already missed out on critical opportunities for learning. The period between two and six years of age is one of particularly rapid growth and development. This is the period when the brain is primed for learning language. If the necessary changes are not made during these early years, the possibilities for learning are not lost, but they may be diminished.

The World of People

Of all the stimuli in the world, the most complex are people. We are social creatures, and the social world moves at lightning speed. When we are with others, we interact using countless subtle movements, gestures, words, and expressions.

Typical children delight in this complexity. Nothing is better than being with other people. They spend much of their time observing and imitating the adults in their lives. They delight in social exchanges that include eye contact and verbalizations. They are eager to capture an adult's attention and take part in the simple games and activities of everyday life. That's why peek-a-boo is such a staple of childrearing. These experiences serve as building blocks for developing language and a host of other cognitive and social skills.

For children with ASD, the social world is vastly different. It is much harder to control and predict than almost anything else. Avoiding people and tuning them out is the best defense.

You have almost certainly experienced this response. Think for a moment about your last several interactions with your child. Try to recall some of the things you instinctively did and said and what your child did in response. These might include

- making a request (which your child did not complete)

- asking questions (that your child did not answer)

- offering affection such as hugs and kisses (that your child did not seem to notice, did not reciprocate, or responded to in a minimal way)

- requesting social behavior, such as "Say bye bye to..." (that resulted in a minimal response or sustained silence)

Each of your overtures is offered with the best intentions. But from the child's point of view these kinds of stimuli are best blocked out.

Resistance: The Child's Defense

Unfortunately, each question, command, or display of affection that is avoided reinforces the child's pattern of tuning out the world. Your child is practicing and strengthening a behavior called *resistance*. Resistance is the child's avoidance of attempts by others to intrude into his or her world. Resistance is a concept that is central to understanding the child with ASD. It also explains why a satisfactory bond does not emerge despite the best efforts of the parent.

Resistance is the child's way of keeping others from intruding into his or her world.

Resistance is something that almost all parents and professionals have experienced in working with a child on the spectrum, and yet it is almost never discussed. Some view it as "taboo" because it seems to suggest that the child is choosing to be defiant. But failure to even consider the possibility of resistance does the child a much greater disservice. It means that the only possible source for the child's difficulties is a lack of ability. When faced with the question, "Can't he or won't he?" adults often choose "can't." Children with ASD are too often labeled incapable when, in fact, what they are showing is resistance. All people, when overwhelmed, will resist. Children on the spectrum are no different.

The Need for Stimulation

Although children with ASD actively avoid much of the world around them, they still seek stimulation. Human beings need *some* stimulation. A total absence of stimulation is extremely stressful. We literally go out of our minds. This explains why solitary confinement is experienced as one of the most severe forms of punishment. In the absence of stimulation, the brain malfunctions and begins to hallucinate—hearing, seeing, and feeling things that are not actually present. The levels of stress experienced from the lack of stimulation are harmful to many systems of the body.

Children with ASD seek a steady flow of stimulation, but it has to be tolerable. Self-stimulation—or "stimming"—fits this bill. Here the child engages in repetitive movements or behaviors such as flapping, spinning objects, repetitively turning light switches on and off, or pulling items out of a drawer. This pattern is so common that it has been viewed as a "core symptom" that is inherent to the syndrome of autism.

Diane at age three pulling clothes out of drawers.

Stimming is an excellent coping mechanism for dealing with a non-hospitable environment. It meets the demands for stimulation but in a form that is manageable. The actions are easy to perform and can be carried out by capitalizing on objects that are always available. Bodies, hands, and eyes are ever-present. Other household items, like strings, light switches, or toy cars, can also be used for the same purpose. They provide low levels of stimulation that are within the child's own control.

The Consequences of Withdrawal

Unfortunately, the child's stimming creates an enormous barrier to most forms of interaction and learning. A bond cannot be created and new skills cannot be mastered when much of a child's energy and attention are aimed at keeping the rest of the world out.

The child, of course, does not know this and does not wish for this to happen. The child is simply trying to reduce unpleasant experiences while, at the same time, avoid a state of complete stimulus deprivation that is equally painful.

When viewed in this light, it is clear why coaxing a child to do things (or not to do things) by using rewards, like cookies, candy, or high fives has little impact in the long run. In the larger scheme of things such rewards are trivial. They cannot change the fact that the world continues to be a difficult place. No cookie or piece of candy can be as rewarding as the security provided by self-stimulatory behaviors and disengagement from the outside world.

The Right to Intervene?

Should we allow the children to stay in their own world? Some have argued that this is the right approach. But for parents faced with the tremendous responsibility of ensuring their children's growth and development, this is hardly an option. All children, whether neurotypical or ASD, *must* receive and accept social input from others in order to develop.

If children with ASD are to master the skills that will allow them to live and flourish in the real world, the patterns of resistance, self-stimulatory behavior, and tuning out must be changed. That change is not simple. It has to be arranged in a slow, meticulous manner that allows them to acquire a sense of comfort in a foreign world.

. . . .

FREQUENTLY ASKED QUESTIONS

How can I tell if my child has hypersensitivities?

Listed below are just a few of the ways that your child may be demonstrating his or her discomfort with the sensory environment:

- showing sensitivity to everyday noises by covering the ears, crying, or avoiding certain settings;
- becoming unusually upset or irritated by particular sounds, such as people coughing or a baby crying;
- withdrawing from hugs, kisses, or other physical affection;
- seeking out certain types of sensations, such as deep pressure, but avoiding others;
- appearing to tune out and be unaware of what is happening in the environment;
- becoming easily overwhelmed or upset when confronted with many different types of sensory stimulation;
- avoiding other people altogether.

For more information, see *The Out-of-Sync Child* by Carol Kranowitz.

Do sensory "therapies" work? (e.g., weighted vests, brushing, deep pressure, etc.)

Every child is unique, and it is helpful to consult with a trained professional to see if sensory therapies are likely to be useful to your child. Sensory therapy is aimed at modifying sensory perception. It often does not require active participation by the child; therefore, it can be started prior to beginning this program.

My child has other symptoms that I think are causing discomfort—severe eczema, allergies, and abdominal discomfort. What impact do these have?

Medical issues like these can be an additional burden. A child who experiences discomfort from the skin, the nasal passages, the stomach, or other parts of the body is likely to have even more difficulty coping with the external environment. It is important to see a physician with expertise in these areas if you feel that your child is having symptoms. Vision and hearing must also be carefully evaluated by professionals.

My child loves hugging, kissing, and other physical affection. This doesn't seem to fit with the pattern you describe.

Many children on the spectrum come to accept physical affection over time as it becomes a predictable part of the routine. It serves as a source of stimulation, much like their repetitive behaviors. Sometimes children use physical affection as a way to escape from more difficult demands. As one parent observed, "Jonathan has a lot of energy but enjoys table work with breaks. He does not have any aggressive behaviors. In fact, his preferred method of avoidance behavior is to give hugs." In order to change this pattern, our program postpones physical affection until the last thirty minutes of the day. This period is referred to as "child-led exchange," and the child may choose to display as much physical affection as he or she likes. (Chapters 5 and 9 address this in greater detail.)

✏️ A Suggested Exercise for Analyzing Your Child's Responses to Your Initiations

Videotape yourself in everyday interactions with your child. Aim for a variety of settings, such as eating, playing, and teaching.

When you have some free time, watch the video (either alone or with a supportive partner) and fill in the chart below.

Adult Initiation (A=Action, D=Direction; Q=Question)	Child responds effectively	Child responds ineffectively	Child offers no response

It is useful to repeat this exercise over three or four days. Then start combining the figures so that you can calculate the percent of time you receive an effective response, an ineffective response, or no response. The figures will give you a good sense of the pattern that marks your interactions, and the effectiveness with which your child meets your efforts in reaching out to him or her.

3

The Parent's Search for the "Key"

In the weeks after Diane was diagnosed, we searched for services to help her—speech-language therapy, physical therapy, occupational therapy, auditory training, sensory integration therapy, and more. The list was endless. I could see how each of these might be important, but something still seemed to be missing.

None of the therapies directly addressed how we could rebuild our relationship with Diane. The implication was that the relationship would emerge as her skills improved, but I saw many children who had been through years of therapy, who had the skills that had been taught to them, but still did not seem open or connected to their parents or therapists. We felt this could not be left out of Diane's treatment program.

— Susan Deland

Having seen the child's perspective, we now turn to the parent's view. Many of the parents we meet are focused on providing every therapy that holds some promise of improvement. Because children with ASD have difficulties in many domains, including motor function, sensory processing, language, and others, the pressure to meet all these needs at once is high.

In the focus on the child and what the child needs, it is easy to overlook what ultimately is central to success—that is, the child's relationship with the parent. The parent-child bond takes a back seat as the child's time is spent primarily with professionals, and focus is placed on instituting many different types of therapy as quickly and intensively as possible. As a result, the parent's relationship with the child does not receive the attention it merits. The child seems "out of reach" and no amount of therapy appears to alter that reality. Over time, many parents start to believe that this is an inevitable part of autism.

Early Signs that the Parent-Child Bond is Off Course

Parents often sense the problem from the early months of the child's life. Parents have told us

> *I knew something was wrong, but I couldn't understand what. He seemed closed off to me.*

> *She looked right through me like I wasn't there.*

> *At first I thought she was such a good baby because she seemed to need so little from me. Then I realized she just wasn't interested in anything I could offer.*

The sense of disconnectedness has been recognized since the early twentieth century when Leo Kanner, a psychiatrist at Johns Hopkins University, first described the condition. The parents that Kanner worked with described their children as being "like in a shell," "happiest when left alone," and "acting as if people weren't there...."

In some children the distortions in the bond are present from birth. In others, such as Diane, they occur at a later point—sometime during the first three years of life.

Susan's note: Diane was an animated infant
who loved to gaze into my eyes

But by the age of two and a half, she
had stopped connecting with me.

The difficulties with communication in children with ASD tend to be one of two types:

- Many children display a pattern of minimal interaction. They are content to be left alone and are often described as being "easy" babies. The interactions with the parent are relatively few in number, resulting in a parent-child relationship that lacks the necessary sequence and flow.

- Other children appear uncomfortable and hyper-vigilant. They demand endless attention and generally receive it. However, the attention and care do not seem to lessen the problems. In these cases the rate of interaction may be greater than usual, but it is generally stressful for both partners.

Methods of Coping

No parent gives up. Instead, they develop ways of coping with a troubled bond. Below are examples from families that we've worked with.

Trying to ensure that the child immediately receives what he or she wants. The child's remoteness can put the parents on edge, leading them to search for the key that will make the child more available. Many parents tell us that in granting the child what he or she wants, they get a glimmer of contact. To keep that going, they do their best to meet all the child's desires. This may be in the form of cookies, television, swinging, and other items and activities. The unstated but powerful driving force is the hope that super-responsiveness from their end will entice the child into a bond that leads to greater engagement.

Asking many, many questions to fill the empty space.
When one partner is not contributing to a relationship, a natural reaction is to fill the resulting gap with lots of one-sided language. This occurs even though the comments and questions go unanswered. Since silence can be unnerving, this feels like the right thing to do. At the same time, the parent hopes to provide the child with verbal stimulation. Unfortunately, spoken language is often perceived by the children as unpleasant, leading them to tune out even more.

Doing whatever it takes to avoid tantrums. All babies cry and fuss, but within a few months, most are able to calm themselves and signals of distress diminish greatly. For many children on the spectrum, this does not happen. In fact, as they grow older and stronger, they begin to cry more because of the distress they are experiencing with the world. The pain of hearing a child cry and scream can be unbearable, and so naturally parents go to great lengths to prevent it. They engage throughout the day in efforts at soothing by providing desirable materials like those noted above (e.g., snack foods, high-tech electronics, a steady stream of videos, etc.). There is also the repetition of seemingly pleasurable actions, such as going up and down in elevators or visiting a particular store. Children who cry at night may immediately be brought to the parents' bed.

Allowing hugging and kissing to become a dominant form of interaction. Affection is one of the joys of life. For parents of children on the spectrum, displays of affection such as hugging and kissing often become even more important—they are viewed as signs of a bond with a child who otherwise seems unavailable. Over time, this pattern can escalate and begin to dominate the relationship.

At first some children shy away, but over time many accept it. The children come to realize that the displays of affection are predictable, require little effort on their part, and therefore are "safe." Though it is difficult to believe, this pattern ultimately interferes with the child's growth. It expands to fill the interaction so that there is little room for other meaningful patterns to develop within the child's repertoire.

Leaving well enough alone. Many children on the spectrum find ways to occupy themselves for long periods of time. This allows them to escape from the outside pressures that they find to be so stressful. Because attempts to reach the child can be extremely frustrating, the parents allow the child these long periods of isolation. Although short periods like this can be beneficial for all children, long periods of this type are not productive. For children on the spectrum, it means staying in their own world, and that ultimately makes it even harder for them when they have to adapt—as they must—to the world they have been escaping.

What Does All This Mean for Intervention?

The patterns just outlined above enable a parent to cope with an extraordinary situation for which no one is prepared. They also demonstrate a depth of commitment that is inspiring. Yet, just as the child's coping mechanisms are not ultimately productive, neither are these. They drain the parents' psychological and physical resources and do not help the children gain the abilities that are within their potential. They do not pave the way for the solid bond that the child needs in order to flourish.

The social sciences have long told us that a child's relationship with the parent or other primary caregiver sets the foundation for all subsequent relationships in life. Not surprisingly, research studies have shown that the effectiveness of intervention for children with ASD correlates with the level of parental involvement: the stronger the involvement, the more effective the therapy. This reflects the fact that the parent is actively remolding the relationship and, in so doing, has created a vehicle for reaching and empowering the child.

Many programs lead parents to take a different path. The setup is designed so that the work is put into the hands of the professionals, with the parent at home having minimal, if any, involvement in the teaching. Home becomes a place where almost all demands are off. The end result is a chasm between the relationships in therapy and the relationships in the family. The already difficult social world for children with ASD is made even more puzzling for them.

As one mother told us,

> When Jason was first diagnosed with autism, I remember feeling as though my primary role was to schedule his therapy appointments. I felt as though I was being told to "step aside and let the experts take over"—that my relationship with him was secondary. One thing that is so refreshing about the Spectacular Bond program is that I now know what I do matters. It's very empowering, confidence-building, and comforting at the same time.

Susan's Experience: Recognizing the Temptation to Push Too Far

Our church has a great Sunday class for children that is low key and geared for fun. Once Diane's behavior improved, we asked if she could attend. The staff happily agreed. Each week, we brought her there and then watched what was going on—to make sure Diane was not crying or complaining. To us, she seemed to be adapting to a new setting, and we felt this was a sign of progress.

When we told Dr. Blank about this experience, she said it would be useful to video Diane in the class and then view the footage together. We did this, and within a few minutes of starting the video, Dr. Blank noticed that Diane had retreated into a corner, adopting a posture of someone trying to hide. She said it seemed like Diane was overwhelmed. As soon as she pointed out the behavior, we could see it, too.

We recognized that we were always looking for signs that Diane could handle the same things as other children. In our zeal for progress, we were constantly testing her to see signs that she was indeed moving in that direction. The class at the church was one of those tests and we didn't let ourselves see the negative impact it was having.

A few years later, when she was truly calm and comfortable, Diane was able to attend and enjoy the class. We learned a valuable lesson. We recognized that certain social experiences we wanted for Diane—church, birthday parties, family gatherings—might be sources of stress for her. We had to protect her from this and trust that the time would eventually come when she could enjoy them without feeling anxious or pressured.

Reflections from Dr. Blank

In my many years of working with children on the spectrum, I've paid particular attention to success stories—those cases of children who have made dramatic and surprising achievements. What did they have in common? It did not seem to be the content of the program. In fact, the techniques varied enormously. Some parents relied on mainstream programs while others entirely invented their own methods. I wondered how so many different approaches could be effective. Was it a matter of finding the right approach for a particular child? Or was something else going on?

Gradually, I began to see a pattern—a theme shared by all these success stories. That theme was an intrepid parent who, against great odds, found a way to create a solid bond with the child. Among the shared features in these cases were parents who had

- the ability to be keen observers of their child and make steady adjustments that took account of the child's sensitivities and strengths;

- a determination to prevent the child from tuning out for long periods;

- a pattern of consistently imposing demands that the child was required to meet;

- an unrelenting confidence that the child was capable of achieving more than he or she was showing;

- the conviction that they were the ones with the power to bring about meaningful change for their child.

I realized that this special bond held the key to success, and that it would be most effective and powerful if put in place at the outset of intervention. Once in place, it would serve as the foundation on which all other learning could take place.

A Final Comment

The two most important people in the bond are the parent and child, but there is a third member that has the potential to contribute something important—the professional. A psychologist, neurologist, or therapist is often closely connected to both the parent and child and can contribute knowledge to help put the bond back on course. The next chapter takes a look at the "doctor's view" and what neuroscience can tell us about effective approaches to treating autism.

. . . .

FREQUENTLY ASKED QUESTIONS:

My child is currently in a program that doesn't have this focus. Can I continue the current program while I begin the Spectacular Bond program? If not, how do I switch over?

There is no need to make any immediate changes. Once you have read through this book, take a week or two to review the different therapies your child is receiving. Part 3 of the book provides guidelines that can help you determine whether other therapies and programs should be maintained or discontinued.

I have a wonderful therapist. Can she do the program?

Yes. Therapists, babysitters, and other care providers can be involved. They should also read this book and become familiar with all aspects of the program.

I'm on board, but I don't think my spouse will be. Can it still work?

As with all parenting, success is more likely when both parents are on the same page and agree to support each other and follow the plan of action as closely as possible. However, the program can be done by one parent as well if the other is willing to take a back seat for the time being and allow the program to be put in place. It can also be a great help to have the support of other family and friends.

How will my other children react?

In general, siblings are the biggest supporters of the program. Once they see the difference it makes in their lives, they are enormously grateful. One ten-year-old boy wrote the following about his sister:

After describing the first two weeks of a difficult adjustment, he said, "It was like rain for two straight weeks, then the sun started to come out. I was surprised. Shocked. Stunned. She is recognizing things. Speaking more. She is even social. Not only did it improve her. It also improved me. I realized that even if she is autistic, I can still love her. I can relate to her now. "

Suggested Exercise

Videotape yourself in a typical ten- to fifteen-minute play session with your child. Set up a video recording device at a distance, perhaps perched on a table or chair, where your child is not likely to notice it. (A phone, iPad, or small camera may do the trick.) Try to forget that the video camera is on and act as you normally would. Later, watch the video and observe your style of interaction. In the chart below record the number of times within a session that you gave a command, asked a question, made a statement, or showed affection. Then use that information, in combination with the suggestions in this program, to determine what behaviors you want to maintain and which ones you want to change.

	Number of Commands	Number of Questions	Number of Statements	Number of Displays of Affection
Session 1				
Session 2				
Session 3				

4

New Possibilities

Tapping into Neuroscience

Autism emerges from a cascade of problems, and with careful and persistent effort many parts of this cascade may be reversed.

— Dr. Martha Herbert, Harvard Medical School, *The Autism Revolution.*

When Susan's daughter Diane was diagnosed with autism, less than ten years ago, the common view was that the symptoms of autism were insurmountable. Most professionals had been trained to believe that autism was a permanent and irreparable condition. Problems with the brain, especially conditions like autism that began in early childhood, were believed to be unchangeable and lifelong.

That view has changed dramatically in recent years, and the new outlook is far more positive than it once was. Starting in the middle of the twentieth century and steadily gaining momentum, neuroscience research has made major discoveries showing that the brain is far more malleable than

.iginally thought. We now know that in autism and in many other conditions it can change in highly promising ways.

Yet, the brain is not quixotic. It does not change on a whim and it does not change easily. The modifications require careful and persistent effort, but with such effort extraordinary change is possible. That inspirational concept is central to the objectives and techniques of this program.

Brain Networks

The only thing that is constant is change.

—*Heraclitus*

The brain is a physical structure, and like every other physical structure in the body, it can change. Think of the bodies of athletes and how different their appearance and abilities are relative to average people. Those differences are the result of both biological components, such as genetic inheritance, as well as environmental components, such as hours of physical training.

In this respect the brain is no different. Its structure and function are affected by many factors—a key factor being environmental input (that is, the perceptions and experiences that an individual continuously receives from the outside world).

Just as exercise affects muscle cells, perceptions and experiences affect brain cells. These brain cells, called *neurons*, are the basic units of the brain, and they connect with one another to form intricate networks. The networks are often described as the brain's "wiring."

What has been shown again and again is that the wiring is not permanent and unchanging. Rather it is continuously being molded by the input that an individual receives—or does not receive. The brain can, in fact, be *rewired*. New connections are created and old connections are removed ("pruned" away) on a continuous basis.

The images above can give you a sense for how different brain areas are connected through complex networks.

Where and How the Brain Changes

Through modern technology, we now have the ability to look deep into the brain and observe the changes that take place. Using these technologies we can see that hours of training devoted to a specific activity—such as playing a musical instrument or learning a foreign language—leads to growth in those areas of the brain that control the activity. By growth, we mean real growth. For example, in musicians brain areas involved in sound processing and the control of hand movements are larger than in non-musicians.

This phenomenon has been observed in other groups of people with unique skills, such as Braille readers (where the networks involved in tactile perception are enlarged) and in London taxi drivers who have trained for years to know by heart every street and tourist attraction in the city (and have enlargement of brain regions that function in memory and spatial awareness). In essence, intense, focused training leads to fundamental changes in those areas of the brain that are engaged in those behaviors. The areas do not start out that way. They become that way through training and do so at a relatively rapid pace. Changes can be detected even after a few months.

What This Means for Children with ASD

From our point of view, what matters most is whether the brain in children with ASD can show similar changes. Are the problems "hard-wired" or can they change with the right intervention?

Neuroscientists have recently begun to try to answer this question by looking into the brain changes taking place. One study published by Geraldine Dawson and colleagues in the *Journal of the American Academy of Child and Adolescent Psychiatry* found that early intervention in young children with ASD led to fundamentally different patterns of electrical activity in the brain. Those patterns looked strikingly similar to the patterns of neurotypical children. Although this area of research is quite new, the early findings show that the brain networks of children with autism can change in significant ways with the right training.

Findings like these have major implications. They suggest that with relevant, concentrated, and sustained input, children with ASD can develop and access the neural networks for many key skills.

There is a major challenge, though, that has to be overcome before changes in the brain can take place. Most children with ASD are not fully receptive to intervention because their attention is tied up in other activities. They spend a considerable amount of their time and energy engaged in repetitive behaviors, such as hand flapping, twirling strings, tearing paper, spinning wheels, lining up objects, scripting, and so on.

The end result is that larger, stronger neural networks are being created in areas of the brain that should not be growing. At the same time, the child's resources are not being directed to those areas of the brain that should be growing, such as the social centers and the language centers of the brain. For effective development to take place, counterproductive patterns of behavior currently in place have to be unseated before new productive patterns can be put in their place.

This situation is challenging, but change is possible if we

- diminish those repetitive behaviors that are working against positive brain growth and

- expand neural networks for those skills that will allow the children to live full and productive lives.

Maximizing the Effects of Intervention: Lessons from Neuroscience

At their core, all intervention programs represent efforts to reshape brain networks. However, not all interventions are created equal. Findings from neuroscience tell us which components are most likely to achieve maximum impact.

Calm the Brain before You Stimulate It

We all know what it's like when our brains get overloaded—from stress, from too much stimulation, from lack of sleep, and a host of other sources. In such a state, we feel that we just "can't think straight." Our focus and attention are deeply compromised.

This state of stress and inattention is one that we frequently see in children with ASD. Teachers and therapists rightly view it as a major obstacle to a child's learning. Stress is also one factor that can lead children to retreat into a world of stimming. Many programs attempt to get children to stop stimming by either asking the child to stop, offering rewards for stopping, or explaining why the behavior is not acceptable. These techniques are rarely effective because a key source of the child's stims—stress from the outside world—has not been addressed.

As Ido Kedar, a young man with ASD, tells us

> Stims have a force that is powerful and compelling.... They come into my mind so suddenly. Then I feel overwhelmed by the urge to do something like hand flapping, or noises, or spitting out water....I treat stims like a welcomed friend because they are really with me all the time. I am so needy to escape reality and stims take me to another world. (*Ido in Autismland*)

Typical techniques have nowhere near the force to compete with the pulls that the child is experiencing. In place of focusing on what we would like to have happen, we need to view the world through the child's eyes. Since stims are a way to escape reality, efforts to lessen stims should focus on modifying the child's reality.

Most intervention programs do not take this approach. Many try to get the child to stop stimming and focus on another activity by offering the child a piece of food or a toy. Unfortunately, this type of approach is only a temporizing measure and does not build the type of sustained calm and focus that is needed for higher learning.

A state of calm focus can be cultivated. It starts with reducing the types of brain activity that are preventing the child from focusing. This type of brain activity can be thought of as "noise"—that is, signals that are not geared to the task at hand. These signals can interfere with the creation of new brain networks and make it harder to access networks that already exist. Stress is a major source of noise.

> *Reduce the noise and chaos, and the brain will increase its bandwidth and access its networks more fully.*
>
> —Dr. Martha Herbert, *The Autism Revolution*

This goal represents a great challenge because children with ASD find so much of everyday life—its sounds, sights, and sensations—to be both complex and stressful. In fact, the greatest difficulties come from people. It is incredibly taxing to process the flow of input that comes from other people. These include rapidly changing facial expressions, gestures, and voices. This can lead to both confusion and anxiety.

Reducing stressful stimulation at the beginning of intervention is the exact opposite of what most programs do. Most programs aim first to stimulate the child in the areas that need development. The major source of the stimulation comes from a person—the parent, the teacher, or the therapist. That person talks, asks questions, presents activities, and is a source of enormous sensory stimulation. In other words the children, when they are still highly vulnerable, are faced with intense contact with people—the very form of stimulation that most confuses and drains them.

The first goal, therefore, must be to reduce the child's exposure to stressful stimulation.

Diane's Experience

Once we were able to change the environment and remove many sources of stress for Diane, we could see a clear change in her behavior. Her facial expressions, her body posture, and her movements were all more relaxed and her stims decreased. We could see her becoming much more comfortable in the world.

When Instruction Begins, Start in the Social Domain

Once a base of calm exists, the introduction of new material can begin. The question is, *"Where* do we begin?" Children with ASD face a range of challenges in many areas that may include language, social interaction, motor function, and sensory processing. Often, in the quest to make things better as fast as possible, all of these are started at once. The children immediately receive multiple forms of therapy several hours each day.

Findings from neuroscience lead us to question whether this is the best approach. We now know that the brain has distinct regions devoted to social functioning. Increasingly, these areas together are referred to by neuroscientists as "the social brain." The social brain is intimately tied to emotional centers of the brain that control feelings of fear and anxiety.

If a child does not have a basic level of comfort with social interaction, any setting in which the child is set up to interact with an adult (which is the case with all forms of therapy) is likely to provoke stress and anxiety. This means that a base of social behavior is the foundation for enabling all other interventions to succeed.

Many programs for children with ASD are targeted at improving the child's social abilities. But in an effort to build social skills, the focus has tended toward teaching what might be better termed conventional "niceties." Great effort is put into getting the children to participate in routine social exchanges, such as saying "please" and "thank you," along with special-occasion requests that we commonly hear, such as "Say good-bye to the doctor."

It's understandable why. These are concrete markers and seem to show that, despite all of their difficulties, the children can still take part in the conventions of everyday social exchanges. What is often unrecognized, however, is that even if the request is met, the children's responses are tiny scattered bits in the vast spectrum of social relationships. As such, they do not help the children grasp the essentials of the interpersonal world. It's as if one is trying to get the child to understand the universe by insisting that he or she recognize the Big Dipper. It's not that it is without value; it's just that by itself, it does not accomplish anything of great meaning.

So how is social ability to be taught? The answer to that question rests in a simple but often overlooked fact—that the social world is not a single, uniform realm but is made up of different types of social contexts.

This fact explains why we behave in completely different ways in the outside world (e.g., a party) and the private world (e.g., a dinner at home with family). It's also responsible, for example, for the different ways in which we respond to a superior (e.g., a boss) and an equal (e.g., a partner). Sensitivity to social contexts is something that neurotypical people display almost each and every minute of their lives with others, usually without giving it a second thought.

Amazingly, that sensitivity is present even in young neurotypical infants. It can be seen in the phenomenon known as "stranger anxiety." Infants begin to respond differently to strangers than to people who are familiar. In other words, they are attuned to differences in social relationships even before they can walk and talk.

Although this realm has been given relatively little attention in some interventions, we believe it holds the key to success. How do we begin to offer children with ASD some insight and skill in this area? Experience has shown us that we can make major inroads by teaching children how to recognize and handle four basic social contexts that are outlined below. With mastery of these four contexts, the children are equipped to handle a wide variety of social settings. These include, but are not limited to, the instructional settings needed for mastery of vital skills such as language.

Parsing the Social World into Four Manageable Social "Contexts"

The real world has innumerable social contexts, and we move easily in and out of different contexts, seamlessly modifying our behavior with little awareness. But for children on the spectrum, this represents a great challenge and a source of considerable stress. At the outset, we can assist them in managing the complex social world by helping them get comfortable in four basic social contexts.

The contexts are:

I **Adult-led exchange**	II **Minimal exchange**
Adult and child are together in the same place and the adult is guiding the exchange. Example: daily activities such as brushing teeth and getting dressed	Adult and child are together in the same place but are not interacting. Example: when parent is cooking, talking on the phone, or otherwise engaged
III **No exchange**	IV **Child-led exchange**
The child is alone. Example: when the child is alone in his or her room	Adult and child are together in the same place and the child is guiding the exchange. Example: when the child is guiding the parent in play time

1. **Adult-led exchange (ALE)**

    This context sets the groundwork for the child being able to learn from adult-led instruction. It occurs numerous times throughout the day when the adult presents activities that the child needs to execute (e.g., mealtimes, bath times, going outside to play, etc.). The goal is to have the child become comfortable and skilled when an adult is guiding his or her behavior.

When the child becomes comfortable here, all other instruction can happen much more effectively.

2. **Minimal exchange (ME)**

   This context is designed to handle a situation that greatly troubles families. It is often expressed in terms such as, "He just doesn't know what to do in his free time." The end result is that parents feel under constant pressure to keep the child entertained. The goal of "minimal exchange" is to enable the child to tolerate *not* being entertained for reasonable periods of time. This exchange offers a huge bonus: it empowers the children to behave quietly and appropriately in non-home settings, such as waiting times in doctor's offices, restaurants, and other locations.

3. **No exchange (NE)**

   This situation is one where the child is alone in a childproof area (usually the child's room) for short periods of time. It may seem strange to place "alone situations" in the context of interpersonal functioning. However, once the child knows that periods of time alone are readily available, he or she is far more ready to accept and cope with the challenges of actual interaction. When parents first hear of this context, they assume it represents "time out," but it does not. "Time out" represents punishment for some infringement. This use is not compatible with fostering social interaction. Rather the goal of "alone time" is different. It is designed to convey the message that the child's room is a haven where he or she can relax and not have to deal with the complexities of the social world.

4. **Child-led exchange (CLE)**

In this context, the adult is present but imposes no demands, requests, or directions. Instead, the child is free to make any reasonable request of the adult. The requests can include stroking, jumping, cuddling, reading books, and the like. They can also include no requests at all. This context gives the child the invaluable opportunity to feel in complete control of the situation.

These four contexts don't capture the full range of social settings that the child will one day need to master, but it is a solid beginning. Later on, children will learn the skills for other settings, such as child-child exchange where they interact with peers. In the beginning, however, this is not essential.

Many intervention programs for children with ASD target just one context. For example, in some programs the children spend nearly all their time in instructional settings where the adult structures the setup and provides a series of directions, leaving the child no opportunity to take the lead. In other programs the child spends most of the day in settings where the adult follows the child's lead, and the adult makes no requests and gives the child no directions. These limitations in the social world leave the child less equipped to handle other contexts when they arise. In our experience, the children are capable of reaching a level of comfort in all these contexts and helping them do so is key to preparing them for the real world.

The Next Step

Now that you are familiar with the key principles behind the program, you are ready to move on to Part 2. There you will find a detailed step-by-step guide to putting the program in place.

. . . .

FREQUENTLY ASKED QUESTIONS:

I'm eager for my child to speak. When does language therapy start?

Once a child shows that he or she is willing and able to follow an adult, other therapies can be introduced. For most children, achieving that behavior takes two to three months. (For more information see the section near the end of the book called *Preview to the Next Step: Teaching Language and Reading).*

My child is in a social program. How is this different?

Most social programs cover skills that are far different than the behaviors we have been discussing. They tend to focus more on conventional niceties than establishing a strong parent-child bond. They also generally concentrate on one context (e.g., child-led exchange) rather than exposing the child to a wider range of contexts.

If my child has little language, how is he going to know what he is supposed to be learning and what he should do?

At the outset, we have found that certain simple non-verbal techniques of communication are more effective than language in conveying to the children what is expected of them. Although children with ASD have limitations in this realm, just as they do in other realms, we have found these non-verbal techniques to be effective. They are described step-by-step in Part 2.

Will the changes you describe make my daughter more anxious and overwhelmed?

One of the important but under-appreciated advantages of social mastery is that it serves to reduce the children's anxiety. It enables them to understand what others are doing and to predict what others are likely to do. Thus, the changes you will make in the program are very likely to reduce your child's anxiety. Diane Deland expressed this idea perfectly when she told her school advisor, "I used to be nervous, but I'm not anymore!"

PART 2

Getting Started
A Step-by-step Guide

An Introduction to Part 2

Success depends upon previous preparation, and without such preparation there is sure to be failure.

— Confucius

Six Key Elements of the Spectacular Bond program

1. Simplifying the World

2. Building Self-Control

3. Managing Meltdowns

4. Sitting Quietly

5. Organizing Daily Life

6. Moving On

The six elements of the Spectacular Bond program are all aimed at a single goal: achieving inner calm and control. That is a great challenge for children on the spectrum, but it is essential for almost every aspect of development. The objective is for the children to feel calm and in control both when they are alone and when they are interacting with others.

Many programs do not aim for this—sometimes because they consider it impossible and sometimes because they deem it unnecessary. Nevertheless, we have seen time and again that it IS possible, and that it is the foundation that enables children with ASD to develop higher skills in language and cognition.

As in any major undertaking, preparation is essential. That's why professionals of all sorts—athletes, chefs, actors, lawyers—devote hours and hours to practicing their skills. Their ambitions pale against yours. You are aiming to achieve the miracle of transforming your child's life.

The preparation for the program involves familiarizing yourself with the six key elements. This means reading Chapters 5 to 10 and then practicing the specific techniques described in each chapter.

This will involve

- rehearsing the techniques alone, with your spouse, or with other family and friends;

- videotaping yourself using the techniques and then watching the videos to see where you are on target and where you can improve;

- filling out checklists that enable you to identify key patterns in your child's behavior;

- rearranging certain rooms in your home so that things flow more smoothly;

- getting organized and creating a daily schedule so that you know exactly what you will be doing throughout the day;

- sharing your plans with friends and family who can provide support. (A note of caution: select your people carefully. Relatives and professionals who are committed to other approaches may be skeptical about what you are planning. Debates about the merits of one program over another will not determine if this program is the right one for you and your child. The only way to know is to begin and give it 100% effort.)

At this point where so much is unfamiliar, this may seem a lot to take on. But you have time. There is no rush. Take a week or two to prepare yourself and hone your skills. The payoff for doing so is enormous.

Once you begin the program with your child, you will initiate the first five elements at the same time. The sixth one begins after the first five are solidly in place. Parents often ask why the first five elements are started all at once and not in a step-wise fashion. There are two main reasons.

- First, putting in place one element often leads to changes in the child's behavior that necessitate other elements. (For example, placing a new demand on your child to sit quietly may lead to a temper tantrum.) It's best if you have the tools to deal with all the difficulties that may arise.

- Second, a step-wise approach leaves the children to face a situation that can be daunting. They find that the "reward" for adapting to one element is the introduction of another whole new set of demands (as the next element is introduced). From their point of view, adaptation in one domain only leads to greater demands. The ante keeps getting raised. Though the aim is to make things easier for the child, from the child's view, the experience is punitive.

By contrast, starting all five elements at once is like pulling off a band-aid quickly. There is a jolt to the child's reality, but within a week or two the child adjusts to the change. After that there are no major jolts. The children see that a new, calmer system is in place and that their world is significantly more stable and predictable.

5

Simplifying the World

Element 1

Because the world is an overwhelming place for children on the spectrum, our first goal is to replace complexity with simplicity. Huge amounts of effort go into stimulating children with ASD, but we are suggesting the exact opposite. Our first goal is not to do *more*, but to do *less*. We are going to reduce or eliminate as much as we can in the environment that may be contributing to the child's stress.

Below are the steps you can take to simplify the child's physical world and social world.

The Physical Environment
Common Areas in the Home
GUIDELINE 1: LIMITING ELECTRONIC DEVICES

For the most part, the physical world of furniture, pictures, and other objects presents no problem. They are stable and unmoving and pose few challenges to the child. However, in modern life there is a component of the physical world that does need attention. It is the high-tech world involving phones, tablets, TVs, video games, and computers. They present the children with high levels of rapidly changing input that can simultaneously attract them and overwhelm them. Many homes that we have visited have TVs on throughout the day. It is critical to change this pattern.

High-tech devices should *not* be available in common areas of the house or in the child's room except for short periods of time (approximately 30 minutes, once or twice per day). Select those periods carefully. They should be used to make your life easier to manage. For example, you might have your child watch TV for 30 minutes while you make dinner.

GUIDELINE 2: MANAGING MEALTIME

For many families mealtimes are a source of stress. (We will provide detailed guidelines for how to handle meals in Chapter 9. For now we are aiming to optimize the physical setup.)

During meals and snacks the child should be seated at a table and not be allowed to move around the room. Some children throw food or wander around while they eat. Your goal is to ensure that this does not happen.

To achieve this goal, it's best at the beginning to have the child eat alone at a table in quiet surroundings. But the child will not be alone. You should be seated close by so that you can act instantly to prevent any counterproductive actions from occurring. You are completely focused on your child at this time and your attention should not be on any other activities.

GUIDELINE 3: MANAGING PHONE TIME

Many parents find that when they speak on the phone, the child's behavior deteriorates. They find themselves shouting at the child, "Be quiet!" or "Stop that!" with little effect.

A solution is to set a schedule so that phone calls take place when your child is not in the common areas of the home (e.g., your child might be sleeping, at school, or at a relative's house). If there is an emergency and a phone call is essential, it's best to have the child in his or her room during the call.

The Child's Room

The child's room plays an important role in the program. The first goal is to set up the room to be a quiet, calm space.

GUIDELINE 4: LIMITING THE NUMBER OF TOYS

Many parents aim to stimulate the child by filling the room with many toys. This encourages the child to engage in short bursts of random activity where he or she moves quickly from one object to the next. It's better to have a small set of toys— five to ten—that are changed from one week to the next. In general, they should be materials that encourage active play, such as puzzles, vehicles, blocks, and musical instruments.

GUIDELINE 5: LIMITING ELECTRONIC DEVICES IN THE CHILD'S ROOM

The child's room should not have a TV or computer, and there should be no other electronic devices, such as tablets or video games. The exception is a radio or CD player that can be used to play music if the child wishes.

GUIDELINE 6: ARRANGING THE PHYSICAL SPACE OF THE ROOM

The room should be a place where your child is free to pursue any activity he or she desires, as long as the behavior is not destructive. The room should be set up so that any objects in the room are ones that can easily be removed if the child begins throwing things or displaying other inappropriate behavior. We suggest storing toys in a container so that you can easily move them in and out of the room when necessary.

If destructive behaviors do occur, it is important to avoid issuing directives, such as, "That's not a nice thing to do, please stop." These directives are rarely effective and ultimately convey the message that your words have no power. Physically arranging the space so that you have control when needed is far more effective and is a recurring theme in the program.

The Interpersonal Environment

Changing the physical environment is relatively easy. It involves looking at the external world and deciding which pieces need to be moved, changed, or eliminated. Changing the interpersonal environment is more difficult. It requires looking within and changing longstanding patterns.

One key pattern for many parents, for example, is that they see themselves as providers of appealing and stimulating experiences. Inevitably, this entails complex levels of language, abundant speech, and exuberant emotions that they hope will capture the child's interest. Although rarely recognized as such, what they are offering are bundles of complexity.

When parents realize that this needs to be changed, their first response is, "Then what am I going to do with my child?" Having been set in one pattern for some time, they find it hard to imagine alternatives.

We believe the better goal is to repackage yourself so that you present a picture of minimal complexity. This involves two domains: (1) the physical cues you give off (nonverbal cues such as posture, gestures, and facial expressions) and (2) the language that you use.

Physical Cues (Nonverbal Behavior)

No parent needs to be told that interacting with a child on the spectrum can be stressful. That stress can be dramatically reduced by changing your own behavior.

GUIDELINE 7: SIMPLIFYING YOUR NONVERBAL BEHAVIOR

Your first goal is to achieve the ability to convey calm even when you may not be feeling it. You may recall Susan's description of Dr. Blank's calm demeanor as Diane screamed during their first visit:

> Dr. Blank brought Diane next to her, sat her down on the floor, and kept her from getting up by holding her firmly at the shoulders. Right away, Diane started screaming. Alex and I stared in disbelief as Dr. Blank did nothing to stop Diane's screaming. She did not try to distract her or comfort her. At the same time, she would not allow Diane to get up. Diane's crying was unnerving to us as it always was, but we were reassured by Dr. Blank's calm manner. No other professional we had met seemed so at ease with Diane.

The subtleties of nonverbal behavior are often difficult to capture in words. In this regard videos can be extremely helpful. Consider, for example, the film *To Kill a Mockingbird*. In that classic movie set in the South in the Great Depression, Gregory Peck plays the widowed father of two young children doing his best to raise them in a strong and principled home. (To see clips of the movie, go to www.youtube.com.)

As you watch the character, you sense almost immediately that despite all the enormous pressures, he will never lose control and can always be relied upon. He achieves this through low-key, slow-paced movements and a soothing voice, even when he is facing situations that would cause most of us to lose our cool.

In aiming to transform your behavior in this direction, you will find it enormously helpful to film yourself with your child. Then during a quiet period, sit down either alone or with someone you trust and watch the video. It will give you the opportunity to examine the nonverbal behavior that is so critical to the interaction. This includes the pace of your movements, the quality of your gestures, and the tone of your voice.

GUIDELINE 8: CONSTRAINING DISPLAYS OF AFFECTION

One of the most important nonverbal realms involves displays of affection, such as hugging, kissing, and stroking. It is hard to imagine that this could ever be counterproductive, but it often is. Understandably, at the outset, most parents that we work with do not see it this way. Instead, they feel that these forms of contact are among the few positive behaviors that the child displays. Once they take a step back, however, they begin to see that often this is not the case.

Many children, for example, use this type of contact as a source of stimulation. They rub their parent's skin, pull on their parent's clothes, or grab the parent's face for a kiss. Eventually this becomes an easy source of stimulation that leaves them with little need for any other input. Affection can also be used as a means to escape teaching. Instead of completing a required task, the child runs to a parent for hugs and kisses.

Physical affection is a vital part of the parent-child relationship, and it plays a key role in the program. But if it is to work for the child and benefit the relationship, limits need to be set. In this program affection is limited to the period of child-led exchange at the end of the day (described in Chapter 9). That is the period when the child is in control and can do anything he or she wants other than be destructive. If the child chooses to use this period of time at the end of the day for affection, it is fine and should be encouraged. But in other settings, it should not.

Some parents have described to us their experience with this aspect of the program:

> We found it hard to limit our affection toward Sean. It made us feel sad. It seemed counterintuitive to deny him affection for even a minute, let alone most of the day. But this sadness disappeared when we saw him wanting to interact with us in lots of different settings. My husband and I were no longer subject to his constant demands anymore. We were parents starting to have a relationship with our son. It was awesome.

> Personally, the hardest thing for me about the program was to limit affection at the beginning. I needed many reasons and a lot of explanation from Dr. Blank to grasp this concept. Otherwise, it would have been a deal breaker for me. I came to see it in this way—for affection to be meaningful and comforting to Jordan meant that I first had to become someone he acknowledged, someone he could understand and feel comfortable with. Only then could affection have real meaning for him.

Language (Verbal Behavior)

In trying to get a handle on language, it's useful to categorize the key ways that we use language to communicate. Although we can literally say millions of different things, everything we say is basically expressed in one of three forms:

- Commands (e.g., "Look at that rain!")

- Questions (e.g., "Is it raining?")

- Comments (e.g., "It is raining.")

In speaking these are constantly intermixed, but each serves a very different role.

GUIDELINE 9: USING COMMANDS

Commands are a language form in which a response is almost always expected. For example, when someone says, "Please give me that box," he or she expects to be given the box. The appropriate response to a command is often an action. A verbal response may accompany the action (e.g., "Here it is."), but it is typically not required.

For children who have language problems, commands are a good form to use when eliciting interaction. However, care should be taken in how and when they are used. Commands should only be used when you can ensure that they will be followed.

One way to do this is by giving a command only when you are within reach of your child, so that you can ensure that your words are heard and your presence is felt. In the early stages if you offer commands when the child is even a few feet away, it is almost certain that the command will be ignored.

In addition to being physically close, it is helpful to make actual physical contact by taking the child's hands into yours, waiting a few seconds, and then speaking. There is no need for the child to make eye contact. The hand holding is a wonderful way of making your presence felt so that it is harder for the child to tune you out.

At the same time, you do not want to overwhelm your child with commands. You offer as few as possible. At the beginning this should be no more than 15 or 20 over the course of the day. This means that your commands should be limited to the essential activities of daily life. The commands should be simple and focused on one clear objective. This means that you should not request more than one action at a time and you should not elaborate on the command.

For example, imagine that your child is watching TV and it is time for dinner. This is likely to lead you to say, "Turn off the TV and come to the table because it's dinner time." Instead of this complicated mesh of language and actions, you should turn the TV off yourself. Then wait a few seconds. After that take your child's hands and say, "Go to the table." This leaves the child to face a single command and it leaves you in a position to ensure that it happens.

Another key feature is the manner in which the command is stated. In general, with people that are not close to us, such as strangers, we tend to be formal. The words are chosen more carefully and the sentences are better constructed. A request for someone to sit down might be phrased as, "Please take a seat."

By contrast with members of our family, we tend to be informal and relaxed. A comparable request to sit might be, "Honey, how 'bout comin' here next to me?" The words flow into one another without any boundaries, making it hard for the child to actually understand what you are saying. All this means that it is better for the child if you use more formal language and follow certain guidelines:

- Avoid pet names and terms such as "Sweetie," "Honey," "Buddy," etc. If any name is used, it should be the child's name.

- Speak in a clear, slow manner where every word is distinctly pronounced.

- Focus on simple actions related to well-learned routines such as going to the table, taking a bath, or putting on a coat.

- Make no requests for spoken language.

- Concentrate on the desired behavior (e.g., "put on your coat") and eliminate unnecessary verbiage (e.g., "it's cold out, you need a coat").

- Make and maintain physical contact by holding the child's hands or shoulders until the child complies with the request.

- Avoid rewards for the completed action (including praise or high fives). The message you want to send is that these are the expected routines of daily life and not behaviors that deserve rewards.

Use short, simple commands for the essential activities of daily life and then ensure that the child follows through.

GUIDELINE 10: ELIMINATING QUESTIONS

Questions, like commands, indicate that a response is expected. However, a key difference is that questions often require a verbal response. For children with language problems, this can be challenging.

Unfortunately, questions tend to be the form used most commonly with children who have little or no speech. Our intuition tells us that this is the best way to spark a response or get someone's attention. It's not surprising that parents of children with ASD speak to their children predominantly in questions.

If you have any doubt, watch a video of yourself with your child and see the number of times you present your ideas in question form such as, "Isn't that nice?" "Would you like to put on your sweater?" and "How about going for a bike ride?"

A key to progress is to eliminate questions. Doing so significantly reduces the breakdowns in communication that permeate life for children on the spectrum. Some parents are distressed at this suggestion, but the elimination of questions is only temporary. It takes place at the start of the program when the focus is on simplifying the child's world.

Parents often tell us that they've been told that questions are essential to getting their child to think. If that were the case, however, the questions should be met by the child with focused, effective responses. They rarely are.

This becomes apparent when you video some interchanges and note the questions you are asking and the responses from the child. In most cases there is either no response or an "off-target" response. This means that the child is experiencing failure most of the time.

It's hard to exaggerate the value of reducing failure. Occasional errors are not significant, but high rates of failure are pernicious. They send children the message that the world is unmanageable and that mastery is an impossible dream.

Many parents, though skeptical at the outset, are amazed at the changes that take place through modifying this pattern of questioning. They report, almost in disbelief, that the child is speaking much more now that they have stopped asking questions. Changes such as these are but one example of your ability to empower your child.

GUIDELINE 11: EXPANDING COMMENTS

When parents hear the restriction on questioning, it's not uncommon for them to ask, "Does that mean we can't talk to our children?" This response shows the extent to which "talking" and "questioning" are—incorrectly—seen as equivalent.

Questioning is not the only way of talking to a child. *Talking also includes commenting.* For example, "You look so pretty today!" or "We have to wait here for the bus" or "That tree is so big."

Commenting is actually the form we use most often when talking to others that are more "conversational." Because children on the spectrum are not skilled in conversation, we tend not to use comments with them. But commenting represents a win-win situation. Comments provide the children with excellent language models. If they choose to attend—which they do more and more as they realize that there is no pressure to respond—they learn a lot about how to formulate ideas. If they choose to tune out, there is no accompanying breakdown in communication.

Because we are not accustomed to using comments with non-conversational partners, it takes a bit of practice. One of the most effective ways to practice this skill is to sit in front of a mirror and simply make comments that refer to simple objects and events that are within your view.

For example, you might have a cup of coffee in your hand and say, "This is my favorite mug for my coffee. I know you have a favorite mug, too—you like the one with the bunny." The language is simple, but it goes beyond the naming of size, color, and shape that commonly dominates language programs. The sentences are well structured, the vocabulary is rich, and the ideas are valid. (See the end of this chapter for additional examples of commenting.)

There are some instances in which commenting is not appropriate and silence is preferable:

- when a child is upset, tantrumming, or scripting
- if the child shows signs of stress.

If your child is calm, even if seemingly non-attentive, comments are an excellent source of language stimulation.

A Final Note

We find that most parents are on board with the idea of simplifying what they do, and they are committed to following all the guidelines set out above. But then the strangest thing happens. As they are getting ready to leave the office, they turn to their child and say, "Now, say good-bye to the doctor." This seemingly reasonable, familiar request is a perfect example of an unnecessary command for expressive language.

It also shows how turning theory into practice can be difficult. Don't be discouraged when this happens. Change doesn't happen over night. One parent told us that thinking about her young son as an adolescent or adult helped to motivate her during the program:

> We all imagine kids on the spectrum as exactly that— kids. But these kids grow into adolescents and adults with different urges and desires. Once I started looking into the future and thinking about Matt as an adult, it radically changed the way that I went about things. That little glimpse into the future helped boost the effort and consistency of how I approached the program.

The process of simplifying yourself is similar in many respects to changing your diet or any other habit—all involve altering long-held behaviors that are carried out unconsciously. If you keep that in mind and don't let yourself get distraught when you occasionally fall off the wagon, you will see remarkable changes take place within a few weeks.

. . . .

FREQUENTLY ASKED QUESTIONS:

Is simplification something that I should be doing 24/7?

One of the great advantages of the Spectacular Bond program is that it does not take a lot of your time. The actual periods of interaction with the child are less than 2 to 3 hours per day. As you will learn in more detail in later chapters, the goal is to have 5 to 10 minutes of contact each hour over the course of the day, so that the child does not disengage for sustained periods. The periods of contact include meals, bath time, playtime, taking a walk, and so on. The rest of the time you will not be focusing on the child. While the guidelines for simplification do apply throughout the day, in practice you will only be actively implementing them about 10 minutes each hour.

If I want to ask my child something, like what he or she wants to eat for breakfast, what should I do?

Rather than asking a question, simply show your child the two options. If you like, you can say what the two options are, for example, "We have cereal and pancakes." Wait for your child to respond either verbally or by reaching for one of the boxes. This method can be used for other choices that the child may make throughout the day, such as choosing what shirt to wear or what toy to play with. If no preference is indicated, simply provide the child with one of the options.

Can I ask certain questions, such as "Do you need to go to the bathroom?"

There is no need to ask. If you think your child might need to use the bathroom, take him or her there.

If I make these simplifications, will my child get bored?

By simplifying the physical and interpersonal environment, you are removing certain types of lower-level input to create space for higher-level input. Initially, there may appear to be less activity taking place, but soon this is replaced by self-directed activities. In other words, boredom (if it is occurring) turns out to be a positive as it leads the child to turn inward and figure out what to do with his or her time.

As the child's behavior improves, you will also begin to provide more productive, structured teaching (described in Chapters 10 to 12). The process of simplification removes much of the low-level, external stimulation that has filled the child's world. This leads the child to tap into his or her own motivational system.

If my child does not respond to a comment, should I repeat the comment?

Commenting is not offered with the purpose of getting a response from the child, so there is no need to repeat the comment if the child does not respond.

If my child does not follow my command the first time, should I raise my voice? Should I continue to hold his hands? Do I repeat the command?

When giving a command, your tone of voice should be firm and calm but not loud. Louder volume, especially shouting, is disruptive and conveys a lack of control. Your goal is to appear—and ultimately to truly feel—calm and controlled. You may repeat the command once if needed but not more than that. You should continue to hold his or her hands until the action is carried out. If you find, at the outset, that the commands are almost never met, then eliminate commands (to the extent possible) for the initial period of the program.

For activities requiring multiple steps, how do I give the commands?

Give one step of the command, wait until it is carried out, then give the next step. For example, when giving the child a bath, separate each of the commands to, "Go to the bathroom" (wait until the action is completed), "Now take off your clothes" (wait until the action is completed), "Get in the tub," and so on.

Does it matter how the command is worded? For example, should I say, "Pick up the toy" or "You should be picking up your toys now"?

Commands should be made in the simplest and most direct form possible. "Pick up the toy" is an example of a direct command, whereas "You should be picking up your toys now" is an example of an indirect command. An indirect command is embedded in other language and is more difficult for children to understand. These should be avoided at the beginning of the program.

How do I speak to my other children?

Some of these techniques can be useful with typically developing children as well, but in general, you should continue speaking to your other children as you normally would.

How do I respond to my child's scripting?

The goal is not to reinforce or reward scripting, so in general it is best to ignore it. We will consider this question in greater depth in Chapter 6.

 Samples of Commenting

At Breakfast:

(Point to pancakes) "Today I made you pancakes. I know you love pancakes, and I hope you love these."

"The pancakes taste very good, or at least *I* think they taste good."

"First I'm going to give you two pieces." (Give your child the pieces.) "See, here's one and now here's two. But there are a lot more over there (point). So if you want more, there's more here for you."

"Wow, you finished all your pancakes. I thought you would do that and that's exactly what you did."

"Now, you know what we do every time after we finish eating. We always wash our hands, and that's what we are going to do now. Let's go to the sink."

(At the sink) "See, here is the tap for getting out the water. Right now no water is coming out." (Hold child's hand under the non-running tap.) "See, not a drop of water."

"Now, I'm turning on the water. It has to be the right temperature. It can't be too cold—oh that is too cold. It can't be too hot, either. Now let me fix it. Now it's just right."

"Now we have your hands in the right place, but we don't have the thing we need to clean your hands. We need soap, and here is the soap. Now I'm putting soap on your hands. Soon they are going to be clean. There, they are clean. Now, let's go and dry your hands."

During a play activity making toy sandwiches:

(Show a picture or a photo of a sandwich.) "Right now we will make my sandwich. I don't want just anything in my sandwich. I want some special things. I want tomato—and here is the tomato." (Put tomato on the bread.)

"Now I want something more. I have tomato and now I want to add lettuce. The lettuce can go right on top of the tomato, right here. So now I have two things on my sandwich, and they are just the things I want. This is great! Now we have to put something on top over here. We can put some bread..."

At the park:

"Wow, it's a beautiful day today. I feel so happy when the sun is shining and it's a great day. It's definitely a nice day to be at the park."

"I'm surprised there aren't more people here. Oh, there are some kids over there. They look like they're having a lot of fun on the swings."

"I recognize those kids. I think they live just around the corner. They sure do love the swing set. I wonder if they're going to get off and give some of the other kids a turn. That would be the nice thing for them to do."

"There's a sandbox that has lots of fun toys in it. Let's play over there. It looks like there's a shovel and a bucket. I see a toy truck there, too. I love the feeling of sand running through my fingers. I can use the shovel to fill the back of the truck with sand, and then we can dump it out into a big pile."

"Oh, it looks like the clouds are starting to move in. I wonder if it's going to rain later. We should probably head home then since I didn't bring an umbrella. It can be fun to get stuck in the rain, too. I don't mind being wet as long as it's not too cold outside."

While cooking dinner:

"I'm so excited about what we're having for dinner. I'm going to make a special recipe. Tonight we're going to have pasta with vegetables. I picked the vegetables that we love the most—broccoli and tomatoes."

"First, I have to get the vegetables out of the refrigerator. I usually keep them on the bottom shelf. Yup, there they are. The tomatoes are especially fresh and ripe. I bet they're going to taste very sweet. I can't wait to eat them. The broccoli is also extra fresh."

"I have to wash them to make sure all the dirt comes off and they're clean. I think they taste best when they're cut into bite-size pieces, so that's what I'll do."

"Now, let's see what kind of pasta we have in the cupboard. I think I'll use the angel hair pasta. I just love the way it tastes and I love the texture. This is going to be a really great meal. I hope you have a big appetite!"

6

Building Self-Control

Element 2

When David stims, I don't know whether I should try to stop him or if it's something he needs to do. Sometimes it bothers me so much I'll shout at him or hold him to try to make him be still. He might stop for a few seconds, but then he starts up again. I don't think the stimming is good for him, but it seems on some level he needs it as an outlet.

— Mother of David, six-year-old with ASD

The simplification of the child's world that we talked about in the last chapter is a top priority. By itself, though, it does not automatically turn things around. For one thing, the children have longstanding patterns of behavior that keep them from attending even to the simplified world you have created.

The most common of these behaviors are "stims" (repetitive self-stimulatory behaviors such as hand flapping and spinning) that so often dominate their attention. For progress to take place, children must break free of these patterns. To do this requires a level of self-control that enables them to keep stims from governing their lives.

When we raise this idea, we often hear parents say, "But we thought that wasn't possible. We've been told that children on the spectrum can't control their impulses." Over and over again, our experience has shown us that they can.

This does not mean that the situation is straightforward or that self-control is easy to come by. It also does not mean aiming to eliminate all stims. We have to begin by understanding that some of the children *do* need stims. They are the main defenses they have for coping with a world that they experience as overwhelming. At the same time, unless the child learns to control these behaviors, they will serve as obstacles to effective brain development.

Still, a solution is possible. It rests in abandoning an all-or-none view. In its place, we need a world of co-existence where both stimming and self-control of stimming reside—just at different times and in different places. This chapter is aimed at achieving that goal.

Managing Self-stimulatory Behaviors

The repetitive behaviors that comprise the world of self-stimulation emerge in a variety of forms. They may involve movements of body parts (such as hand flapping) or they may involve objects in the world (such as repetitively pulling on strings). Any action that a child can readily perform can become the basis of a stim. Regardless of the particular form it takes, the behaviors share common features:

- they are entirely within the child's control and

- they help the child tune out the world.

The combination provides the child with a level of comfort that is desperately needed.

Carly Fleischmann, a young woman with ASD, tells us

"Stims are when you make or create output to block sensory input or overload. It's a way 2 shut down all my other senses & just focus on one."

The abundance of stimulation that surrounds us is something we take for granted. Indeed, in many cases we hardly even notice it. For example, most people do not sense the clothing they are wearing. It just fades into the background, far from awareness. For children on the spectrum, the ever-present clothing, like so much other background input, can elicit continuous, unbearable sensations. Stimming is the child's answer to the problem. It creates an intense focus that enables them to block out a wide range of other input.

The price they end up paying, however, is enormous. Having found a level of comfort, they feel little motivation to do anything else. As a result stimming serves as a phenomenal force for dampening development because it keeps the child from the encounters with the external world that are necessary for learning. At the same time, efforts to completely remove stimming result in the children feeling overwhelmed and unprotected.

A balance is needed where stimming is still available as a resource for the child, but at the same time limited so that it does not dominate the child's life.

Helping the Child Achieve Self-Control through "Controlled Exchanges"

The key to success rests in what we term "controlled exchanges," which allow the children to slowly and systematically alter their behaviors. At first, the periods of control are brief, occupying only some seconds of time. These ultra-short periods of time are critical in enabling the children to feel that the situation is tolerable.

At the same time, the encounters are regular and consistent. Much like the way that running water carves out new channels in rocks, the new interactions carve out new channels of behavior. As the behavior improves and as new, more effective patterns get established, the control is steadily expanded.

To give you a sense of the type of behavior that will be targeted in a controlled exchange, we'll start with a sample scenario.

> *Max is a five-year-old boy who often occupies himself by pulling books off shelves. This happens several times each day. When he does this, his mother tells him to stop. Not surprisingly, he does not listen, and he continues pulling the books. Hoping that consequences will matter to Max, his mother tells him to pick the books up and put them back on the shelf. Sometimes this leads to a struggle as Max ignores the request. Sometimes he picks up one or two books, leaving the rest for his mother. But regardless of the consequences, there is no reduction in the book-pulling behavior.*

Having identified this unproductive behavior, Max's mother can now take the first step toward changing it. She sets up an interaction with Max that has one clear goal in mind:

> *To get Max to look at the books for a short period (about 20-30 seconds) while resisting the urge to pull them off.*

In other words, Max will be led to put in place a brief period of self-control. From this small beginning, greater and greater periods of self-control can be achieved. This is accomplished through the "controlled exchange."

A sample controlled exchange is described below:

Max's mother selects a time when Max is not overly tired, upset, or bothered by other problems. She sets aside 45 minutes for the controlled exchange, knowing that in the beginning it may take this long to achieve even some seconds of self-control. For the full 45-minute period, she and Max have nothing else to do and nowhere else to be, and no one else is present in the room.

She stands next to Max near the bookshelf. As expected, Max begins to reach for a book. As soon as he does this, she immediately takes hold of both his hands. Holding his hands in hers, she then shakes her head, "No," and continues to hold his hands to prevent him from reaching for a book. Max is surprised. He screams and tries to get hold of a book. His mother remains calm and quiet. She continues to hold his hands to prevent him from reaching his goal.

Seeing that he cannot get to the books, Max tries another tack—he attempts to get away. If his mother lets him go at this point, nothing will have been achieved other than an unpleasant experience for both partners. So his mother steadfastly holds on, even as Max's resistance intensifies.

A few minutes pass and Max's mother senses a slight easing of Max's resistance. He is quieter and not pulling as fiercely to get away. The mother then gradually lessens the strength of her hold.

As soon as she does this, Max tries to reach for the books again. His mother was prepared for this and she reasserts control by again taking hold of his hands.

This pattern of holding and releasing continues until Max, without being held, stops reaching for the books for a period of about 20 to 30 seconds.

This end point to the controlled exchange is determined not simply by time. It also involves body language where Max's posture and facial expression clearly convey acceptance on his part. For many parents, that body language may be new and surprising. Its appearance represents one of the great benefits of the controlled exchange. In this clear, focused situation, the child is able to—almost pulled to—see the parent in a new light: a light where the parent is calm, resolute, and effective. That powerful experience opens a channel into the world of social interaction. The children are capable of a far wider range of social skills than they typically exhibit. However, the interaction has to be carefully crafted for this to happen.

> *Max's mother is acutely aware that she must not overly stress Max. The situation has been demanding and anything more will be too much for him to handle. So knowing that Max has given his all, his mother takes him to another setting—a setting with no books—where both of them can relax.*

GUIDELINE 1: IDENTIFYING UNPRODUCTIVE BEHAVIORS

Take some time to observe your child and make a list of unproductive behaviors. Behaviors to target include

Body stims
Hand-flapping
Finger flicking, twisting, or tapping
Pacing or running back and forth
Snapping fingers
Picking at fingers or another part of the body
Thumb sucking
Body contortions
Licking body parts or objects

Moving fingers in front of one's eyes
Rocking or spinning
Rubbing body parts or objects

Stims with Objects
Turning light switches on and off
Opening and closing doors
Dumping objects out of bins, drawers, or cupboards
Twirling, dropping, throwing, or mouthing objects
Flipping the pages of a book
Pulling books off shelves or taking objects off counters and
tables
Eating non-food items
Pushing buttons

Note: when the stim involves objects, you have the choice to
hold the object (e.g., hold a door that the child is trying to open
and close) or to hold the child. Either is fine and you select
which option you want, based on what you find easiest to do.

Stims using other people's bodies
Hitting other people
Touching or rubbing up against another person's face or
body
Pulling on others' clothing
Kicking

Self-destructive behaviors*
Head banging
Biting the arms
Smacking a hand against something, including oneself

*Many self-destructive behaviors resolve through the techniques
indicated here. However, *all self-destructive behaviors should be
discussed as soon as possible with a physician or other professional*

who can provide devices, equipment, and techniques that will prevent significant injury.

These stims are some of the more common ones, but your child may display others that you should also target.

Criteria for which behaviors to target

Target only those repetitive behaviors that occur on a sustained basis. If a child displays a repetitive behavior for

    (a) less than 30 seconds at a time and

    (b) less than 5 times per day,

it should be ignored.

There is one class of behaviors that you should not target: *vocalizations*. You do not have the power to stop what a child expresses through sounds and words. In general, you will find that excessive vocalizations diminish when internal control is established for other behaviors. In addition, as in the scenario above, you'll be using very little language during the controlled exchange. You may find that your diminished verbalizations lead your child to lessen his or her inappropriate language.

GUIDELINE 2: TARGETING ALL THE BEHAVIORS AT ONCE

With the list created, parents often ask if they should focus solely on one behavior at a time. When one behavior improves, they plan to move on to the next.

While this seems reasonable, it does not work well. From the child's point of view improvement seems to lead only to more demands. Their reaction is, "Why bother cooperating?

It makes things harder, not easier." By contrast, if all the behaviors are targeted at once, the transition is made quickly and progress is far better. The first day or two will be difficult, but within a few days, the child understands the full range of what is expected. This enables the child to feel more secure. With security comes greater cooperation.

GUIDELINE 3: BYPASSING REWARDS

Rewards such as candy, toys, high fives, or effusive praise are not part of the controlled exchange or any part of the program. This may be surprising since rewards often play a powerful role in other programs.

Despite the widespread use of rewards, they do little to help the child progress. A major reason for their lack of long-term effectiveness is that they shift the focus of the activity to the reward and away from the adult. The hope is that the reward will motivate the child and engender positive emotions that the child will then connect to the person providing the reward. Despite its widespread use, the children do not make this connection. As a result, the reward does not lead them to feel greater interpersonal connection with the adult.

The key to change rests not with rewards but with reframing the relationship. Your child needs to see you as a calm, comprehensible person who has the power to bring him or her into your domain. You must become someone whom the child accepts as a guide through a difficult journey. That is the foundation you are starting to build at this point.

GUIDELINE 4: CREATING A WORKABLE PLAN

1. *Setting aside the necessary time*

    Once you are in a controlled exchange, you need to follow through. This means having 45 minutes set aside to carry out the exchange. You may not need all this time, but you should have it available in case you do need it. Although the 45-minute period is by no means easy, many parents find it helpful to know that there is a clear end in sight.

When the exchanges are handled in a consistent way from the very beginning, the time it takes to achieve your goal usually decreases quickly. Within a few days, there will be a noticeable improvement. Self-control is established quickly once the child gets the message you are sending.

It is a fact of life that there will be times when you cannot devote 45 minutes to a controlled exchange. This may happen, for example, if you are leaving for work in the morning and your child starts pouring toys out of bins. In these cases the best course of action is to act as if you are ignoring the behavior and "pretend" that nothing has happened. (Later on, you can rearrange the space so that this won't happen again in the future. This can be done, for example, by keeping bins of toys out of your child's reach.) Although ignoring the behavior does not serve to teach your child self-control, it is far preferable to telling your child to stop and then being unable to follow through. That sends your child the message that your words have no power.

2. *Limiting the number of controlled exchanges*

In general, you should aim for three to five controlled exchanges in a day. These should be distributed over the course of the day, and you should try to avoid more than one in any hour.

If you find that the child's behaviors occur far more frequently than five times per day, you should limit the number of controlled exchanges by

- ○ Structuring the environment so that the behaviors occur less frequently. This can be done by removing objects that provoke stimming. In the case of Max, for example, it would mean moving books to shelves that he cannot reach.

- ○ Acting as though you did not see the behavior.

- ○ Having your child go to his or her room on a more frequent basis so that there will be fewer opportunities to stim in the presence of others.

When your child is sick, you should not engage in any controlled exchanges. When your child is well, you can resume.

3. *The quality of the exchange*

The controlled exchange happens almost entirely without speaking. Instead of using words, you will use body language and facial expressions to convey what is needed. You should aim to have a "poker face"—the expressionless face of a good poker player that conveys calm control. If you feel that you must use some language, limit it to a few phrases, such as "please don't," "please stop," or "not now."

4. *The length of the exchange*

You will need to exercise some judgment in deciding how long your child must control himself or herself in order for the exchange to end. In the sample scenario, we suggested starting off with a goal of 20 to 30 seconds of control. This works well for many children; however, there are some children for whom self-control is more difficult. For them, five seconds of control may be all they are capable of in the beginning.

The length of the exchange should be determined by how the session has progressed up to that point. For example, if you have been working at the exchange for about five minutes and your child shows good self-control for a period of 30 seconds, you might choose to aim for a somewhat longer period of 60 seconds.

On the other hand, if you have been carrying out the activity for half an hour and you finally get 10 seconds of control, that is sufficient. Though brief, it is a definite segment of self-control and you should not ask for more. In other words, you tailor your goals to your child. Generally, within four to six weeks, the children are able to exhibit self-control for three to five minutes at a time.

As noted earlier, equally important is your child's body language. What you will see, through the child's look and behavior, is an expression of calm acceptance and a relaxation of the tension in the child's body. Sometimes the child begins to look intently at you, trying to figure out how serious you are in your efforts. This scanning to determine your intentions may be something you have never seen before. Though it is subtle and brief, it represents a significant step in remaking your relationship. You are no longer being tuned out; instead, you are becoming someone that the child needs to notice and understand.

When the child becomes calm, the hold is gradually released. *It is only in the period after the release that the child can learn what is needed.* While the child is being held, he or she is not learning self-control. Once the position is released and the child has the opportunity to move, that is when self-control can begin.

If the child tries to resume the behavior, you immediately reassert control by taking hold of the child's hands. If the child does not try to resume the behavior, but instead remains calm for the desired period (e.g., 30 seconds), then the controlled exchange comes to an end.

In the beginning the child will almost certainly try to resume the behavior each time the hold is released. In this case the cycle of releasing and then reasserting control repeats several times. As it does, the child begins to perceive that this is a two-choice situation. Either he controls himself or the parent controls him.

In our experience this is the first time that the children are faced with a decision of this sort. Nevertheless, because it is so clear, they almost always recognize it within a few minutes. As the expression goes, you can "see the wheels turning." It is under these conditions that self-control begins to develop.

After several cycles of release and repositioning, the child will achieve the targeted period of control. The exchange then comes to an end. By ending the exchange when an acceptable period of calm has been achieved, the parent conveys to the child the message that she recognizes the limits in the control the child is capable of at this time, and she will never make demands that exceed the child's capabilities.

Presenting the child with two-choice decisions (other-control vs. self-control) is helpful in establishing clarity, and clarity is an unbelievable ally in your quest to gain your child's trust and cooperation.

5. *After the encounter*

Because the encounter is likely to be stressful for both you and your child, it's best to follow it with an activity that relieves tension. Some excellent options are described below:

a. *Physical activity (e.g., going for a walk, jumping on a trampoline, etc.)*

There is considerable research to indicate the stress-relieving value of sustained physical activity. One of the best activities you can carry out is walking with your child.

At the outset, it is important to structure the activity so that you don't find yourself in an uncomfortable position, such as being far from home with your child screaming and refusing to walk. To deal with this possibility, the initial periods of walking should be very close to home, yet long enough to be characterized as "a walk." For example, you might walk up and down your street several times. That way, if your child becomes difficult you can easily get back home.

As the walking routine becomes stable, and your child is clearly cooperating, you can expand the distances. Most children over four years of age can handle a half-mile to a mile walk. During this time it is preferable that you insist that the child hold your hand. Then you are not subject to the child running away or going off course.

b. *Spending time alone in his or her room*

A particularly good time to use the room for rest and relaxation is immediately following a controlled exchange. For children who need to stim to further reduce tension, the room is an ideal place to do this.

They learn that stimming is available to them when they are alone in their own rooms.

If you are going to use the room, do it by calmly guiding your child there for about 20 minutes of time alone. This is *not* a time-out where the room is used for punishment or discipline. Instead, in this program the room serves as a place of respite and relaxation.

When the child is alone in the room, nearly all activities are allowed. They can stim. They can stare out the window. They can line up cars. They can listen to music. In other words, the room offers the children an opportunity to be free of social pressures.

There is an important aspect of room time that the child *does not* control, however, and that is when it takes place and for how long. You will be the one to determine when your child goes to the room and for what length of time. This avoids the situation of having the child spend excessive periods of time alone in the room, isolated from the outside world.

At first, the children may not recognize the value of the room—particularly if it has been used for time outs. But within a week or two, most begin to realize the treasure they have. It's akin to the relaxation you feel upon coming home from work and sitting down quietly for a period when you can unwind. (Tips for how to make your child's room a safe and relaxing place can be found at the end of this chapter.)

Benefits of the "Controlled Exchange"

When we think of having exchanges with a child, we typically think of activities involving actions we want to have happen, such as the child playing with a toy, catching a ball, or turning off the TV. Our initial focus here, however, is on what is best termed "not doing." Partly this is for practical reasons—it is difficult to make someone do something; it is easier to ensure that someone not do something. Partly, it is for developmental reasons. Not doing what one wants to do lays the foundation for controlled behavior. Self-control is taught by showing the children how they can control their impulses.

The exchange is set up so that control is

- initially established by you (when you hold your child's hands or body or an object to prevent an action) and then

- transferred to your child (when you let go and your child stays calm without trying to resume the unproductive behavior).

In other words, the child has to be in the position where he or she could execute a desire but elects not to. That represents a quantum leap in self-control.

The controlled exchange gives your child several key messages:

- You, as the parent, cannot be ignored even though you are imposing demands that your child may not find appealing.

- You are able to control your child in a calm manner.

- Your demands are firm but tolerable.

- Your child faces a simple two-choice situation— either to demonstrate self-control or be controlled by someone else.

- Your child has the power to manage his or her urges.

Receiving this many clear messages from a single encounter is something entirely new in the children's lives and it has enormous power. It leads them to see the world in a new light. Within a short time, the effects—built over repeated encounters—are extraordinary. But the goals are attained only if the adult has set reasonable demands that he or she is ready and able to enforce.

It's important to remember that the goal is not to stop any and all actions. For example, you would not want to stop productive activities such as a child using blocks to build something. The only time that you would interfere with a productive activity is if the child loses himself or herself in it for hours on end.

It's also important to remember that your goal is to reduce the child's unproductive behaviors, but only when he or she is in your presence. You have no ability to control what the child does when he or she is with others, nor when he or she is alone. Hence, you make no efforts in that direction. Happily, what you are likely to find is that as you establish control, it will transfer to others such as teachers and therapists.

A Closing Note from Susan

I remember taking Diane at age three to a friend's house. In the bathroom there was a beautiful glass bowl of potpourri next to the sink. I remember thinking, "I'll never be able to have something like that. Diane would break it in a second. Within nine months I no longer had those kinds of worries. Diane learned to control herself in all kinds of settings—at school, friends' houses, stores, and even museums. Now I have lots of lovely, fragile decorations throughout my house. Not only does Diane leave them alone, she enjoys their beauty!

. . . .

FREQUENTLY ASKED QUESTIONS:

What do I do when I'm short on time?

As described above, a controlled exchange should only take place if you have a substantial period of time (generally 45 minutes) set aside. If you don't have the time, you should ignore the child's behavior and focus on doing what you need to keep the day on schedule. For example, if you have to go out, focus on putting the child's coat on and getting into the car. Ignoring unproductive behaviors in this manner does not teach the child control, but it does avoid the situation of you making requests that are not followed through.

Can I offer my child a distraction to keep him from stimming?

Your instinct and perhaps your education may tell you to offer a distraction—a desirable alternative activity that will take the child's attention away from the unproductive behavior. Although such an approach may be needed at times in order to prevent the child from self-harm (e.g., providing chewing gum so that the child doesn't chew his lip or fingers), it doesn't help you achieve your larger goal of teaching your child self-control. In other words, distractions may temporarily stop the behavior, but they do not teach the child control.

Distractions can also reinforce unproductive behaviors because the child sees that any unproductive behavior gets you to introduce desirable alternatives. The child recognizes that, "If I do something they don't want me to do, I will get lots of other things that I like." It's a clever realization but not a productive one.

Why do I have to be in close physical proximity to my child?

When you are at a distance, your presence is not felt. At a distance your only tool is language (e.g., saying things such as, "Don't touch the books"). As you have almost certainly experienced over many interactions, that type of language does not work. The only way to achieve your goal is to be close to your child where you can easily establish and maintain physical contact.

What do I say during the controlled exchange?

It is best to say little or nothing. If you feel the urge to say something, say an occasional, "Not now" or "Please stop." It's important that you do not offer any words of reassurance—do not say, "I'm sorry," or, "It will be over soon." Do not have a look of apology or remorse on your face. Such words and actions may make you feel a bit more comfortable, but they send the child mixed messages.

After the controlled exchange, I try putting my child in his room, but he won't stay there. It's the only place where he can relax and I can get some much needed down time. What should I do?

First, ensure that your child's room is safe and that there is no potential for self-harm. Then put your child in the room and close the door. Hold the door closed from the outside and do not let your child open it. If for some reason your child cannot tolerate a closed door, you can get a gate that allows him or her to see outside of the room. Regardless of which option you choose, do not say anything and do not respond if your child says something. When you speak, you are sending the message that the issue is open for discussion. It is not, and it is confusing to have your child think it is. Within several minutes the children understand the situation, and they will generally find ways to occupy themselves in their rooms. Often the end result is better self-directed play—another valuable byproduct of the program.

You've said that we should not target vocalizations. Is there anything that can be done to reduce them?

This is one situation where it might be helpful to stop comments. Comments can foster language, and if your initial goal is to reduce the child's vocalizations, the fewer comments the better. The more silent the environment, the more likely it is that the child will reduce his or her vocalizations.

How do I stop unproductive behaviors when I am not with my child?

The answer to this is simple: you don't. You make no efforts to control stimming when your child is alone in his or her room. The stimming in other settings may diminish, but you have no ability to make it diminish. Keep in mind that if your child learns to control himself or herself in your presence, you will have attained an invaluable goal.

What do I do about my child's unproductive behaviors when we are out of the house?

At the outset, try to avoid public situations where you know the behaviors are likely to occur. In Chapter 11 you will learn how to transfer the program to public settings.

What do I tell the teachers to do at school?

All of the techniques are designed to be used when your child is with you at home. Even if teachers are willing to carry out the program at school, they usually do not have the time, space, or support to do so. You may or may not wish to mention to the teachers that you are starting a new program at home. With young children, what happens at home frequently generalizes to other environments, including school. As a result, you may be surprised that within a few weeks the teacher will report to you an improvement in your child's behavior at school.

My child goes into his brother's room uninvited, and this is upsetting to my other son. Do you consider this to be an unproductive behavior? If so, what should I do?

Yes, this should be viewed as an unproductive behavior. One effective strategy, if you feel comfortable with it, is to allow older siblings to have locks on their doors. Another effective strategy is to keep close watch and prevent the child from entering the sibling's room. If the child sees that all attempts to enter the room are unsuccessful, he or she will likely stop trying.

Regardless of your solution, the goal is to avoid the entry rather than to punish it when it occurs. After-the-fact punishment is rarely effective. Whatever technique you select, make sure that it works to prevent the entry from occurring in the first place.

Can other family members or friends be present during the controlled exchange?

Generally, it's best for the controlled exchange to be carried out without others present. If you feel that you'll need assistance, especially at the start of the program, choose a friend or family member who is supportive and understands the goal of the activity. Select someone who will aid you in successfully carrying out the exchange rather than someone who is likely to prevent it.

Tips from Susan for Making Your Child's Room a Haven

- Choose a pale color for the walls, for example a pastel. Dark and bright colors can be overstimulating.

- Keep bedding colors cool, too, and avoid bold or showy patterns.

- Consider a weighted blanket if your child seeks and finds comfort from deep pressure.

- Keep the walls relatively clean of pictures, posters, and other items.

- Have some soft lighting options, like a lamp with a low-watt bulb.

- An iPod or CD player may be used to play soft background music from time to time. Many ASD kids are drawn to classical music, as it can calm them.

- Designate a nice play area on the rug or at a small table. Have some of your child's favorite toys available nearby.

- Don't have too many toys available, and rotate them weekly to provide variety.

7

Managing Meltdowns

Element 3

Having to deal with a meltdown can be a bit like dealing with earthquakes...you get very little warning and about all you can do is just ride it out.

— Parent of a child with autism
(http://theautismfactor.com/meltdowns-vs-temper-tantrums)

Among the many challenges facing parents, meltdowns are invariably at the top of the list. It's easy to see why. They are overwhelming, disorienting, and discouraging. Quite a lot is written about ways to handle meltdowns once they are underway. Less has been written about how to prevent meltdowns from ever getting started. As with so many of the symptoms of autism, it is assumed that they are part and parcel of the syndrome and, therefore, unavoidable. Nevertheless, our experience with hundreds of families has shown us that this goal is well within reach.

The first step is to learn to distinguish between two types of meltdowns: *tantrums* and *overloads*.

Tantrums versus Overloads

All young children have limits on the resources available to them for dealing with stress. When they are uncomfortable, whatever the source, they tend to exhibit disruptive behaviors and emotional outbursts. As a result, the overt behavior in tantrums and overloads are similar—screaming, kicking, throwing, and the like.

The forces operating in the two categories, however, are not the same. Each stems from different sources and each requires a different plan of action.

In *tantrums*, the disruptive behaviors occur when children do not get what they want.

In *overloads*, the disruptive behaviors occur in response to sensory overstimulation.

We start by focusing on what is needed to reduce tantrums; after that, we move on to strategies for preventing overloads.

Tantrums: Why They Happen

In the many books written on tantrums, a consistent definition emerges. A tantrum is seen as "the action that children resort to when they do not get what they want." This definition mentions only the child, but almost always there is another person present as well. Usually the child has expressed a desire to someone else, and that person has not granted the wish. In other words, to be accurate, the definition of a tantrum should be, "the action that children resort to when they do not get what they want –**FROM THE PERSON to whom their want has been expressed.**" Frequently, that person is a parent.

This shift in how we define a tantrum has major implications for understanding and dealing with the behavior. In place of focusing on the behavior as being entirely within the child, it becomes a behavior that is part of the parent-child interaction. What the parent does is critical.

In our experience parents go to great lengths to avoid tantrums. For good reason. Tantrums are painful not only to the child but to anyone witnessing the behavior. Here is but one example of what can take place:

> Sam was a six-year-old boy with ASD who regularly wanted to ride up and down an elevator that was located in a building a short car ride from his home. It was not unusual for him to wake in the night and request an elevator ride. Regardless of the time, the parents met the request. The alternative was to stay up all night facing a full-blown tantrum. Compared to that, the trip to the elevator seemed easy. Sam's parents said that they never imagined they would go to such lengths to meet his requests, but they were desperate to avoid a tantrum.

Anxiety is not the sole reason that parents grant the child's wishes. Many parents understandably sympathize with the child because of the very real hardships that mark their lives. Granting them some enjoyment seems like the kind thing to do.

Meeting a child's requests is also seen as a way to create a critical opening—a crack in the wall of isolation between the child and others. Parents and therapists are often pleased to see a child making a range of requests. It is seen as the possible start of meaningful interaction. As one parent poignantly said, "The only time I get a sense of contact with Emily is when I give her the cookie that she asks for. That's when she looks at me and sometimes smiles."

The underlying hope is, "If enough desires are fulfilled, maybe the wall will crack and dissolve." For all these reasons, encouraging children to make requests by saying "I want" has become a pillar of many intervention programs. But our experience suggests that the reality is quite the opposite. By teaching children to say "I want," they are led over time to expect that all requests will be met—and met quickly. This is an impossible dream.

Further, the children will inevitably express wishes that cannot be fulfilled. If their expectation is that their wishes will be granted, tantrums are unavoidable. Efforts to reason with them (e.g., "The store is closed. We'll go tomorrow…") are fruitless. Even if they comprehend the complex language being offered, they are in no mood to be reasonable.

Temper tantrums do not occur solely because the child desires something he or she doesn't have. Instead, they have their root in a parent-child dynamic where the parent has established the message that whatever the child requests, the parent will try to provide.

The following excerpt from one of Dr. Blank's articles in the *Huffington Post* has struck a chord with many parents:

> As the children enter adolescence, the issue becomes even more problematic. It then is not simply a failure of language to advance, but a major breakdown in behavior. The children are now bigger and stronger and their wants have expanded—often in realms that even the most giving of parents cannot permit. This leads the parents to deny the requests—a move that leads the children to major acting out, often in aggressive and destructive ways. When viewed from

the children's perspective, this is only reasonable. They have been encouraged for years to believe that the granting of what they want is of the highest priority to their parents. Now these vulnerable individuals see the basic pattern that they have relied on for years being challenged or rejected. What the parents then see is the ultimate outcome of encouraging "I want" language.

GUIDELINE 1: DISTINGUISHING BETWEEN NEEDS AND DESIRES

The first step is to get a clear picture of your child's needs and differentiate them from desires. You will, whenever possible, meet your child's needs quickly. By contrast, you are going to be taking a different path in meeting his or her desires.

When you are in the planning phase of the program, set aside a couple of hours to be with your child and observe what is taking place. Preferably, video the interaction and later watch the video. As you view the behavior, use the chart below to list the requests your child makes. This can involve pointing at a TV, saying the name of a desired object, pulling you over to a particular place, and so on.

Child's Request	Need	Desire

Once you have the list, determine whether the particular request is a need or a desire and place a ✓ in the corresponding column.

Examples of Needs:
using the bathroom
water
food (when hungry)
adding or removing clothing (depending on the temperature)

Examples of Desires:
video games
TV

toys
forms of recreation
unhealthy snacks

GUIDELINE 2: ESTABLISHING NEW PATTERNS FOR NEEDS AND DESIRES

With the distinction between needs and desires now clearly in mind, you are going to create new patterns of interaction. If your child expresses a need, it should be met freely and easily. Moreover, your child should never be required to "use words" in order to get needs met. For example, if a child needs to go to the bathroom, he or she should be able to do so as quickly as possible. It only adds to the child's frustration to have to delay and come up with language to make the request. If the child has communicated the need to you in some way, it should be met quickly.

Desires are treated differently. All children deserve the things in life that they find appealing. The key is to meet a child's desires *without* setting the stage for temper tantrums. The following guidelines detail how to achieve this goal.

GUIDELINE 3: LEARNING WHAT NOT TO DO

Many parents have been told that a good way to handle meltdowns is to provide a distraction. A child who begins to show signs of dissatisfaction and an impending tantrum is to be given a desirable object or directed to a pleasurable activity. Unfortunately, these techniques send the message to the child that any sign of dissatisfaction will be rewarded with something desirable. The end result is a strong message that meltdowns pay off, as they lead to better and better choices.

This may be why, despite the widespread use of these methods, meltdowns continue to be pervasive. It also contributes to the incorrect belief that meltdowns are an inevitable part of life with autism.

There is another common pattern that ultimately works against the child's development. It is based on the belief that the child's desires are a great vehicle for facilitating language. That leads adults to give children almost anything they request as long as they pay a price for it—the price of language. Before receiving their desires, children are required to state what they want. That's why "use your words" is one of the most common instructions that the children hear.

The underlying logic is that if children see that their language is powerful in getting their needs met, they will use more language. This practice is used even with non-speaking children, who are required to use picture boards or computer-based devices to indicate the item they want.

There are unfortunately major unintended consequences to this practice.

One parent of a ten-year-old girl with ASD highlighted one such side-effect:

> At this age we are getting serious behavior issues around her wants not being fulfilled—outbursts of anger, shouting, self harm, destructiveness. It is her expectation that ALL her wants be fulfilled. I have tried redirecting and giving other choices, but now this isn't really working either and sometimes there is no other choice she will accept. I had never thought before that it comes from how communication has been taught to my child.

The child's unreasonable response is actually quite reasonable. She has been taught over many years: "If you talk, you will get what you want." Children on the spectrum are not adept at handling the qualifications that life inexorably imposes (e.g., "but the TV is broken," "if the store were open," etc.). "Ifs, ands and buts" are not anyone's strong suit; they are particularly difficult for those with ASD. So when the desire is not granted, rage ensues. As the children get older and stronger, the rage becomes more intense.

Fortunately, the difficulties outlined above need never arise if wants are handled effectively from the outset.

GUIDELINE 4: LEARNING TO USE TWO POWERFUL WORDS: "NOT NOW"

It's simply not possible to fulfill each and every request that a child makes—even if a parent wanted to. This leads the children to experience inconsistency: sometimes their wants are granted, but other times they are not. Children on the spectrum find inconsistency very upsetting and when they are upset, they tantrum. They know no other way. In other words, inconsistency sets the stage for tantrums. The solution rests with eliminating inconsistency. This, in turn, leads to a guideline that may come as a surprise: **For the child who tantrums when requests are not granted, requests should never be granted at the time the child makes the requests.**

Parents are often shocked by this guideline. Invariably, they take it to mean that the children will never get what they want. In no way is that the case. Your child will continue to get what he or she desires, but you will not be responding to the requests *at the time the requests are made.* Instead, you will be fulfilling those desires at a time and place of your choosing. Essentially, you and not the child will be in charge.

The change from child-directed to parent-directed interaction is powerful. It moves the situation away from a grey area where the child faces a set of complex ideas: "Maybe my request will be granted, maybe it won't. And maybe if it is denied it will be met if I tantrum enough." Instead, the child confronts a clearly defined black-and-white situation that is far easier to understand: "My wants are not granted when I request them. But I can regularly count on my wants being met at times when I am calm."

How is this new pattern to be put in place? The answer is found in a simple two-word phrase: "Not now." This phrase is markedly different from seemingly related phrases such as "in five minutes," "right after dinner," etc.

"Not now" has no implications for future time whereas the other phrases do. As such, those other phrases keep the discussion alive and encourage the child to continue focusing on the desire. Your goal is to put the issue to bed (for the moment) and stop all discussion about it. The two simple words, "not now," are ideal for this purpose. If your child asks "when?" or "why not?" do not respond. Your message is that there is no room for discussion or negotiation.

The following scenario illustrates how this pattern is put in place:

> Sophie is a girl who frequently picks up DVDs and holds them out to her mother, saying, "Play, play." Instead of the typical response of playing the DVD, her mother takes the DVD and places it out of reach. Then she holds Sophie's hands, looks at her, and says slowly and deliberately, "Not now."

The combination of words and behavior conveys to the child that the decision not to grant the request does not stem from inattention, anger, or other negative emotions. Rather, it represents a careful decision that the parent has made. Parents often report that those two little words—"not now"—become their best friend, and within a short period of time, they take on immense power.

GUIDELINE 5: STAYING CLOSE BY TO OBSERVE THE TANTRUM

When you first put the pattern in place, you should not be surprised if your child responds with a tantrum. When this happens, it's natural to feel anxious and perhaps pressured to say or do something to turn things around and halt the tantrum.

Instead, take a deep breath, and *do nothing*. Stay in close proximity to your child. If he or she resorts to unproductive behaviors such as throwing or hitting, then follow the procedures described in Chapter 6. If the child is simply complaining or crying, stand close by while maintaining a poker face.

Many parents tell us that they are used to leaving the room when the child is tantrumming. In general, this is not a good idea. One of the most powerful messages you can send to your child is that you are NOT disturbed by the out-of-control behavior. Unless you are feeling overwhelmed, it's best for you to stay in the room.

Some parents handle a tantrum by putting the child in his or her bedroom. We do not advise this course of action. It's important that you stay with your child and not remove him or her to another location to be alone. Remember, your child's room is to be a haven, not a place of punishment.

Initially the child's negative reaction may take quite a bit of time, but it is unlikely to exceed 45 minutes. If you are consistent, you are likely to see a dramatic improvement in your child's behavior within a matter of days.

GUIDELINE 6: DECIDING WHEN TO MEET THE CHILD'S DESIRES

All children deserve to have things that they enjoy. What you will do is decide the time that is best. If 15 minutes have passed and your child is calm, you can grant the wish. That period is long enough for a young child not to link the request to its being received. This strategy allows you to grant the child's wish without encouraging the child to make requests.

It's also an excellent idea to offer things your child likes when no request has been made. That way, your child sees that when all is calm you are a provider of wonderful things.

This does not mean that you should feel pressured to meet all of the child's requests. The decision to provide the desired item is up to you. For example, if the child has requested a treat, decide whether the child has already had enough treats for the day. If it is for an electronic device, base your decision on how much time the child has already had that day. Generally, it is advisable to limit the total time for electronic devices to one hour or less per day.

Food is a complex area because it can fulfill either a need or a desire. Snacks and treats—like cookies and chips—are desires that do little for nutrition. You should treat them as you do other desires. On the other hand, foods like fruits and vegetables are important for a child's nutrition. If your child has not eaten in a while and requests some food, this should be considered a need and you should provide a healthy food that the child finds appealing. If the child is not willing to eat this food, it's likely that he or she is not truly hungry.

It may seem paradoxical, but you may find that when you offer your child what he or she has been requesting, your child chooses to reject it. Do not be at all disturbed, and do not make any efforts to coax the child to accept it.

A Bonus

The new plan often achieves more than the reduction of tantrums. Freed from a preoccupation with saying, "I want," the children start to deploy their energy in other directions.

They begin to examine other options, such as playing with toys or looking through books.

Parents also find that their child's language expands, and he or she begins to make comments about the world such as, "It's getting dark out." Children who begin to comment about things around them, rather than concentrating on asking for things, have made a huge leap. It is a sign that they are becoming open to learning about the outside world.

Reducing Overloads

Now let's consider the other type of meltdowns—overloads. From all outward appearances, they do not seem to be different from temper tantrums. However, they stem from an entirely different source.

Overloads are not the outcome of a child having requests denied. Instead, they represent the child feeling overwhelmed by the encounters of daily life—encounters that most of us don't even notice. For children on the spectrum, those encounters are experienced as pressures that are difficult and sometimes unbearable.

As Temple Grandin described, "Tactile stimulation for me and many autistic children is a no-win situation. Our bodies cry out for human contact but when contact is made, we withdraw in pain and confusion."

GUIDELINE 7: RECOGNIZING HYPERSENSITIVITIES

Children on the spectrum are often super-sensitive to external stimuli, such as loud noises, or internal stimuli, such as abdominal pain. Ironically, many sensations that are especially appealing to typical children, such as textured foods, bright colors, or distinctive sounds, are precisely the ones that children on the spectrum find intolerable. These are often referred to as *hypersensitivities.* It's impossible for those of us who are not on the spectrum to fully appreciate just how difficult everyday experiences can be.

Your goal is to recognize and avoid input that leads your child to feel overwhelmed. The chart below may be helpful in categorizing your child's hypersensitivities.

My Child's Hypersensitivities

Hearing	Seeing	Touching	Smelling	Tasting
(example: the sound of vacuum cleaners)	(example: fluorescent lights)	(example: wool clothes)	(example: perfumes)	(example: certain food textures)

GUIDELINE 8: INVESTIGATING THE SOURCES OF OVERLOADS

Identifying the triggers for your child's overloads needs to be done carefully. It often requires rethinking established routines that can easily go unexamined.

Videos and journals can help you identify the triggers for your child's overloads. For a few weeks, keep a record of the overloads that occur. The entry can include the day, the hour, and the context—both the immediate one (who is present and what is being demanded) as well as the context that preceded the meltdown. Factors such as time of day and the setting you are in can play a major role in overloading the child.

Diane's Experience

When Diane was three, I was determined to put her in a Halloween costume like the other preschool kids, despite the fact everything about Halloween was difficult for her—shouting kids, scary decorations and noises, scratchy costumes with headpieces, tights and gloves, going out in the cold darkness, and so on.

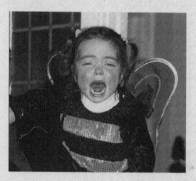

A few years later, her sensitivities were much better, and she started to enjoy Halloween with all the other kids. I regret forcing her to trick-or-treat in those early years, but those early missteps were part of an important learning process for us. We've come such a long way since then.

This process is one that takes time. Whether you use videos, diaries, or other recording devices, it may take a few weeks until you sort out the situations and the behaviors. The overloads may continue during this period. But in taking your time, you are creating the information base that will allow you to identify and change the precipitants.

Once you feel that you have identified the sources of the overloads, the next step requires that you eliminate, to the degree possible, the source of the stress. Because the routines that trigger the meltdowns may be ones that you value, it can be hard to let them go, even knowing that it is temporary.

For example, you may have found that large family gatherings such as Thanksgiving dinners are a key source of meltdowns. This means that your child should not, for the time being, attend those dinners.

It does not mean that you, your spouse, or your other children have to miss the occasion. With babysitting arrangements in place, you can still join the family gathering. Or you may decide that a small dinner for just your immediate family is the better choice for the time being. But the key is that you know what to expect and you realize that you have the ability to decide what is best for you and the rest of your family.

GUIDELINE 9: COPING WITH FAMILY PRESSURES

It may be difficult to convey the message to your family that a new order is in place. So difficult, in fact, that you find it stops you from carrying through.

That is what happened with Randi, a six-year-old boy who had displayed violent behaviors for many years. His father started the Spectacular Bond program and devoted himself untiringly to helping his son. The results were extraordinary. After a year in the program, the boy was calm and content. He was learning to read and write, and he was mainstreamed for some classes.

One day, the father announced that his parents were arriving from overseas for a stay of several months and that he would have to temporarily halt the program. He said that his parents would be living with them and that it would not be appropriate to have strict rules in place during the visit. They expected to be able to enjoy their grandson without restraint.

Fortunately, finances were not an issue and we suggested that the grandparents stay in a nearby hotel or apartment where the child could visit them for one hour a day. That way, the grandparents could enjoy time with their grandson, but Randi's routine at home would not be disturbed. The father said that this would be a great insult to his parents and that he could never consider such an action.

About eight months later, the father came back with his son. With tears in his eyes, he acknowledged that the child's behavior was worse than when we first met. This was not unexpected since Randi was now older and stronger. Although the father made desperate attempts to re-establish the routine, he did not succeed. Eventually, the child was no longer able to live at home and was sent to a residential facility.

The multiple pressures of daily life are indeed enormous. For most families, the first priority is the child. In that case, you need to be firm and not give in to outside pressures. The best course is to explain the reasons for your decision and to calmly maintain your position. Avoid fights and debates. The feelings of others are important, but they pale in comparison to your responsibilities to your child.

Diane's Experience

Diane's greatest sensitivity was to sound—especially loud continuous sounds from large groups of people. One Christmas we hosted the whole extended family for dinner. Diane was completely overwhelmed by the sounds of all the voices speaking at once, the ripping of wrapping paper, the loud laughter, and the motorized toys. I lost track of her at one point, only to discover her in her bed, buried beneath a pile of quilts. The relatives took turns visiting her upstairs, which she responded to a little. Mostly she stayed hidden, waiting for silence to return. Fortunately, in this case she had a place to escape to. Her room was a safe place for her. If there had been no way to escape, she would have certainly had a meltdown. For the next several years after that, we kept family gatherings small with just four or five visitors. That way Diane could take part without being overwhelmed.

GUIDELINE 10: HANDLING UNAVOIDABLE STRESSES

Despite your best intentions, you are likely to find that you cannot eliminate all of the major stressors that are causing meltdowns. Consider, for example, allergy season. Many children on the spectrum experience severe allergic reactions, leading them to be very uncomfortable during certain times of year. Watery eyes, runny noses, and itchy throats are just a few of the symptoms.

During these periods the best course of action is to keep life as simple as possible. In general, maintain the basic routines and discipline. They serve to ground the child and offer a zone of security. *However, you should not attempt new teaching and new activities during this time.* New material requires the expenditure of a lot of resources on the child's part, and when the child's body is under stress, it is difficult to call upon these resources.

The same rules hold when your child is ill, even with what seems to be only a common cold. Children with ASD are generally more sensitive to physical stresses of all sorts. The best approach is to ease up on demands during that time but not to completely eliminate them.

. . . .

FREQUENTLY ASKED QUESTIONS:

If my child is hungry but will only accept a treat, such as a cookie, should I give the cookie?

Your child is actually making two requests. The first is for something to eat (because he or she is hungry). The second is for a specific treat. If a child is hungry, the request for something to eat is a need that should be met. The request for a specific treat is a desire that should not be met at the time of the request. In this instance you could show your child some fruit and say, "You can have one of these." Your child may then choose. If your child does not accept the food you offer, then simply end the interaction. It is far more effective to offer real items, as opposed to the common practice of offering verbal choices such as, "We have apples and bananas. Which do you want?" Verbal choices are difficult for many children on the spectrum.

Some children have extremely limited diets, and parents fear that the children will not get enough calories. This should be discussed with your child's doctor and may require a consultation with a specialist in gastroenterology, allergy, or nutrition. See Chapter 12 for some useful strategies to expand your child's diet.

Will I be disempowering my child by not meeting his desires right away?

We often get this question, and it reflects the power that "I want" requests have been accorded in our culture. Fortunately, the opposite is what usually happens. Meaningful and productive power does not come from making requests and having those requests met. Even more significantly, it does not come from having temper tantrums to get what you want. Meaningful power comes from learning a range of skills that enable the child to handle the world effectively.

Will my child think that I'm not available to her and will she stop interacting with me altogether?

Children on the spectrum, even more than neurotypical children, treasure predictable, safe patterns of interaction. In general, you will find your child interacting MORE with you and interacting MORE FULLY with you as you create clear, simple, comprehensible patterns.

Are there some children who simply aren't capable of learning to control their tantrums? I've been trying different methods with my child for many years now. Some things work a little at the beginning, but nothing has worked long term.

The problems you are experiencing are not likely to have stemmed from your child's inability. Rather, the patterns are ones that have been learned over years. This is especially true in older children. That is why it is important to reach the children as early as possible. This doesn't mean that the methods won't work for older children. It may just require more time and effort.

What do I do if I'm short on time and my child makes a request that, if not met, will lead to a tantrum?

This difficult situation is one that many busy parents encounter. It means that on occasion you have to "give in" just to keep the day from falling apart. If this happens occasionally, it is not a serious problem. Just do your best to resume the appropriate methods as soon as you can.

However, the exception should not become the rule. You need to ensure that you create the time needed to work through the difficulties. It will pay off in the long run and free up a great deal of your time. To the extent possible, try to clear your schedule for a few weeks as you begin to implement the program. If feasible, ask friends and family members to help with daily tasks, particularly if you have other children.

How long does the system for tantrums and overloads have to be maintained?

Generally, if your child is under 6 years old and you implement the program consistently, you will see major improvements within a month. Then you can steadily and gradually ease some of the demands, but overall the pattern needs conscious attention for about a year.

What about my child's "blankie" (or other preferred item)? She's used to having it with her all day. Is this OK or should I take it away because it's a "desire" and not a "need"?

In general, these items can be made available to the child in his or her room for select periods of time, such as nap time and bedtime.

One parent described her experience with this aspect of the program:

Sam's blankie was almost a part of him. He would often sit on the floor, sucking it as he zoned out. We knew we had to do something about this if we ever wanted him to share in our world. The first time we took it away, we showed him that we were putting it in his room and that was the only place he could have it. Even though it was available, he screamed and kicked. It went on for an hour, although it seemed like an eternity. By the next morning, Sam understood that his blanket stayed in his bedroom. I think in some way he felt liberated. He was still able to go into his room a few times a day and have the blanket when he needed it. Soon after we set up this new pattern, he almost always came out and chose to stay outside with the rest of us.

What do I do if my child makes a request when I'm out in public and I know she'll have a tantrum if she doesn't get her way?

At the beginning of the program, it's essential to carry out the guidelines solely in your home or in a place where you are totally comfortable, such as a relative's house. You need to be in a space where you do not feel anxious if a tantrum should occur. So if you know a tantrum is likely in a particular outside setting (e.g., a restaurant), avoid that setting for the time being.

Once tantrums have diminished in the home, you can begin to carry out the guidelines in public places. Chapter 11 describes how to make the transition from home to the wider world. This transition, like all transitions, can be challenging. The good news is that after two or three outside encounters of this sort, the children realize that the same rules hold in and out of the home. With that realization, your life—and the life of your child—becomes remarkably easier. Parents often report that they never imagined the freedom that comes with achieving this behavior.

We want to be able to go to birthday parties, restaurants, and have other special occasions as a family. When we do this, though, my child very often will have a meltdown. Still, I can't help thinking, "Maybe this time will be different."

Even when children begin to settle into the new system at home, they often continue to have trouble with social events outside the home. Birthday parties, restaurant meals, and family picnics are some of the common sources of difficulty. It is in these "occasional" settings that meltdowns are likely to occur.

Eventually, they will go well. But at the outset of the program, follow the guidelines in this chapter and hold off on social events that are likely to lead to a meltdown. It can be useful to recall the old story of the tortoise and the hare. The hare was fast but overconfident. The tortoise, on the other hand, just kept at his task. Despite his slow speed, he won the race. "Slow and steady" is a good motto to keep in mind when you are tempted by the idea "Maybe this time."

What do I do with "needs" that my child repeatedly requests every few minutes, such as going to the bathroom or having a glass of water?

Generally, the first request represents a true need but subsequent requests do not. Use your best judgment to determine whether the second or third request represents a true need. If you decide that it does not, treat it as a desire and respond accordingly.

Now that I no longer meet my son's desires immediately, I feel sad. Are there other ways I can show him my love and affection?

There are many different ways that you can show your child love and affection. Here are a few ideas:

- go on long, pleasant walks together
- provide a warm, soothing bath in the evening with a few enjoyable toys
- sit together quietly in a comfortable setting, enjoying nice scenery or music
- set out healthy treats that you know your child will enjoy (e.g., apple slices, celery sticks with peanut butter and raisins, etc.)

In Chapter 9 you will learn more about the child-directed period each night where your child can take the lead and choose the activities. During that time your child can hug, kiss, and cuddle with you as much as he or she would like.

8

Sitting Quietly

Element 4

In our very first appointment with Dr. Blank, Diane sat calmly next to her without being held or restrained in any way. I had no recollection of ever seeing her this calm for this extended a time. All this in one session! Now I could see how rapid change might be possible.

— Susan Deland

S itting is something that rarely catches our attention. If we think about it at all, it is only in the background of other activities. We sit down to eat, we sit down to watch TV, we sit down to put on our shoes. We rarely sit for the sole purpose of sitting—with one exception.

Meditation

Introducing meditation in a book about young children with ASD may seem strange. Meditation is usually thought of as an advanced practice that requires a high level of insight. Many think of it (mistakenly) as involving sophisticated techniques for achieving a trance-like state. But meditation, at its core, is a simple act—it is the act of being still.

> Sitting meditation is actually very simple. Almost too simple, really. All that is necessary is to be silent and motionless for some period of time, and also to remain awake and alert.... If you sit down, keep your back straight, and keep still for five minutes—you are meditating.
>
> —Zenmind.org

Certain forms of meditation do require advanced skill and training, but that is not our goal here. Our goal is to teach the children to sit quietly for a period of up to ten minutes. Doing so brings a sense of calm that most children on the spectrum rarely experience. That calm, in turn, sets the foundation for enabling them to engage in a range of activities from participating in family outings at restaurants, to learning to read, to sitting in a mainstreamed classroom. Mastery of this single behavior has untold benefits.

Still, many parents have told us that they cannot allow themselves to even dream of behavior like this. They are used to seeing their child in constant motion, moving from activity to activity. Aside from the counterproductive periods of zoning out, they cannot imagine the child sitting quietly for even a few minutes. Then we remind them that they've actually seen it happen. For example, many children who are viewed as unstoppable sit quietly when playing a computer game.

It's clear that sustained sitting is possible for children on the spectrum. The difference now is that the child will be sitting quietly under the parent's direction. This change has critical consequences in what happens to the child's mind.

Calming the Mind

For children on the spectrum, the information of everyday life is often experienced as a flood that is too much to bear. This includes conversation, traffic noise, television, or children running and shouting on the playground. There is no doubt that relief from this constant input would offer extraordinary benefits. The problem is, "How do we get this message across to young children, especially when they seem caught up in their own world?"

This is where "quiet sitting" comes in. Clearly it is not meditation in the usual sense, where an individual consciously adopts a mind set to observe the steady flow of mental activities. However, sitting does by its very nature reduce much of the flood of information assailing the child. It limits the information coming from both external and internal sources. The end result is the creation of pathways to a unique experience of calm that the children come to value.

Research has shown the power of calming the brain. Patterns of electrical activity in the brain change noticeably during meditation. Individuals who meditate long-term can show lasting changes in brain activity, including increased activity in regions of the brain associated with sustained attention and concentration.

Although "quiet sitting" is not as profound as meditation, you will see firsthand in your own child the potent effects it can have. Once the children experience the state of calm it offers, many of them begin to request it.

Reframing the Relationship

Beyond its role in calming the mind, quiet sitting enables you and your child to reshape your relationship. It truly is a quiet time; nothing else is going on. This gives your child the opportunity to focus on you and see you as a person who is calm and controlled. At the same time, the activity provides a structure that they come to find comforting.

From the children's point of view, you are controlling what they are doing, but the demands are super easy. This enables you to be simpler and less demanding than you have been up until this point. The child sees you in a new light—as someone committed to the relationship as well as being committed to moving slowly without taxing the child's resources. There are few opportunities for interaction with the children that offer these benefits.

Preparing for Individual Differences

Depending on the child's level of resistance, the period to achieve quiet sitting can vary from about two to twelve weeks. As one example, it's useful to consider Diane's case. Although she sat readily for Dr. Blank in the first appointment, changing the patterns at home proved more difficult. This is only to be expected. Dr. Blank was starting from scratch, whereas the Delands were altering already established patterns. That is always more challenging.

As Susan describes,

> When we first started, my husband and I took turns from one session to the next. For both of us, she thrashed wildly, screaming in rage. Anytime she tried to get up, we held her down. It took an enormous physical and emotional toll on all of us. On some days the session ended with me and Diane dripping in sweat. We knew from other parents who had done the program that our progress was slower than theirs.

Then one day, during a session with Alex, Diane let out a nasty scream followed by a fierce glance at him. Since her autism emerged, Diane had never used her eyes to communicate with another person. Her gaze was generally fixed in the corner of her eyes or she stared blankly ahead. This was a major breakthrough.

Alex rushed to me with tears in his eyes. "She actually looked at me!" he said. Diane had returned from her planet to ours for a brief moment. The moment lasted a second, but it energized us in ways that are hard to describe. After six weeks, she was able to sit quietly for up to ten minutes at a time, and we began to see more rapid progress in all her skills.

GUIDELINE 1: SELECTING THE TIME AND PLACE

Choose a time of day when you and your child are well rested and alert. At the outset you should have at least 45 minutes of free time. In the beginning it might take this long to achieve even a few seconds of quiet sitting since your child does not yet understand this activity and may resist. Once the behavior is established, it will take far less time (somewhere between two and ten minutes).

The sitting should take place in a quiet room but preferably not the child's room. The child's room should be reserved for relaxation and should not be used for structured activities.

Have two chairs facing each other, one for you and one for your child. Both chairs should have a firm seat and back. Your child's chair should be small enough that he or she can sit comfortably with both feet on the floor. If this is not possible, put a box or stool under the child's feet for stability. The room should be free of distractions, and the door should be closed with no one else present.

GUIDELINE 2: INITIATING THE ACTIVITY

To start the activity, go to where your child is. Remove any objects that the child is playing with. Stand behind your child, place your hands on his or her shoulders, and say, "Go to the chair." Do not push or lead your child to the chair, but simply wait.

It may take a few minutes, but if you are calm and persistent, the child will generally move to the chair. Every bit of active compliance such as this indicates that the child is adapting to our world, however tiny the steps might be. If at the start your child does not elect to move to the chair, you can gently lead him or her to do so.

GUIDELINE 3: ARRANGING THE APPROPRIATE POSITION

Have your child sit down with both feet firmly on the floor, hands resting lightly on the knees, sitting upright. Take a seat in the chair facing your child with the same posture. Sit close enough so that you can hold your child when needed.

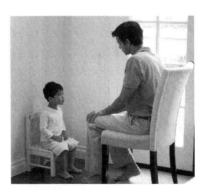

The overarching goal of this activity is to achieve silence and stillness. Therefore, restrict all extraneous behaviors, such as kicking the legs, moving the arms, twisting the head, picking the nose, and so on. You can accomplish this by gently but firmly holding the parts of the child's body that are moving.

If your child makes any vocalizations, put your finger over his or her mouth, shake your head no, and say nothing. Resist the urge to say seemingly calming words such as "It's just a few more minutes," "Almost done," or "No talking." One of the most effective ways to restrict vocalization is the indirect one of reducing the amount of language you use. At the beginning the more silent the exchange, the more effective it is for your child. Efforts to restrict vocalization may not be successful. If they aren't, simply ignore the behavior.

GUIDELINE 4: DETERMINING THE PERIOD OF TIME

Your goal at the outset is approximately 30 seconds of quiet sitting. However, this can be challenging for some children. If your child actively resists this activity, the two of you are likely to be exhausted after 15 or 20 minutes. Should this occur, aim for just a few seconds of calm acceptance from your child. How will you know when this has happened? The child's expression will be similar to the one described in Chapter 6 during the controlled exchange. What you are looking for is a brief but definite pause in the child's resistance and a slight relaxation. Once you see this, end the activity.

Aim for at least one, but preferably two periods of quiet sitting each day. Once the child is able to sit quietly for a few seconds, steadily increase the time by 15 to 30 seconds each day until the child is sitting calmly for up to four minutes.

Once your child can sit for four minutes, there is a change in the daily pattern. Rather than steadily increasing the time (as you have done up until now), instead vary it from session to session. For example, have your child sit for three minutes one day, six minutes another day, two minutes another day, and so on.

Once you are at the stage of varying the time from day to day, set the minimum at two minutes and the maximum at ten minutes. By varying the periods—in this as in many other activities—the children gain flexibility and are freed from the rigid patterns that so often characterize their lives.

GUIDELINE 5: ENDING THE ACTIVITY

To end the activity, say, "You can get up now." Give the instruction in this way—as an indirect statement rather than a direct command (e.g., "Get up now"). Why? If you give a direct command and your child chooses not to follow and instead stays seated, you are faced with a potential struggle (where the child maintains his refusal) at a time when your goal is to end the activity. The indirect statement allows you to achieve your goal. You have signaled an end to the activity, and the phrasing of your message gives your child the choice of getting up or continuing to sit.

Do not offer any praise and do not do anything to help your child get up. You may be surprised to find that your child continues to sit quietly. It's almost as if the child is saying, "Now it's under my control, and I'm going to stay here." Your child might also stay seated because he or she is not accustomed to indirect statements and is unsure what to do.

If your child remains seated, stay nearby but do not stay seated. Without any explicit direction, your child will eventually get up—usually within a few minutes. When your child does get up, do not allow him or her to run away. It is important that all behavior surrounding this activity be carried out in a slow, calm, purposeful manner. If the child is acting without control, have him or her sit down again, hold the child in that position until the child is calm, and then physically assist the child in exiting the activity in a calm, controlled manner.

. . . .

FREQUENTLY ASKED QUESTIONS:

I can't imagine my child being able to sit quietly for that length of time. Are all children with ASD capable of doing this?

Most parents start out in a state of disbelief. Parents have told us

"Quiet sitting felt hopeless during the first few attempts, but it was amazing how fast he understood what was expected of him."

"After the second session, he knew exactly what to do. I was really surprised how calm and collected he could be."

"I was SHOCKED that my child could do this. I think the key to this for us was starting off with tiny increments of time. Once he knew the drill, he actually starting enjoying this exercise."

"Quiet sitting seemed impossible at the beginning. It was difficult but we stuck with it and things improved within a week. I was surprised he could do this. We still use this technique four years later. It helps calm him."

Is it unfair to make my child sit quietly?

The opposite is actually the case. Not teaching children this important skill makes things much harder for them in the long run. As you will see, this quickly becomes a positive activity for both you and the child. It also has transfer value to other settings such as school. Parents commonly tell us that the children are sitting quietly in circle time for the first time.

My child is too strong for me to control his movement. What do I do?

This is an important concern, and it can be handled in a number of ways. If a member of your family is stronger than you, this activity can be handed over to that person.

You can also make some adjustments to the procedure. For example, you might want to start by having your child sit on the floor. This is generally an easier position than holding the child in a chair.

If your child is over six years of age, you may find it difficult to put this activity in place. As studies have found, changes in behavior are easier to implement in children six years and under. For children ages seven and older or for children who are physically too strong to restrain, seek the guidance of a professional to determine whether or not this can be safely implemented at home.

9

Organizing the Day

Element 5

The activities we've been considering so far occupy only a small part of the day. As your child's behavior improves, the routines become smooth and difficulties get resolved more quickly. The activities then occupy an even smaller part of the day. That leaves parents to raise a key question, "What do I do with my child the rest of the time?"

Mainstream intervention programs often answer that question with four words: "The more, the better." The thinking behind this approach is clear. The children are seen to be in urgent need of stimulation, so it seems logical to offer as many hours of intervention as possible. Anything less than the most is insufficient.

The approach does not go unchallenged—with the challenge usually coming from school districts or health systems which face financial constraints. Under pressure to limit expenditures, they often refuse to support the extensive array of services that parents request. That typically leaves families to take on enormous financial burdens as they try to provide all possible services to their children.

There are actually far better reasons for being conservative about the provision of services. *What is far more important than financial concerns is what is best for the child.* Sustained hours of one-to-one interaction can be overwhelming for children on the spectrum. Their ability to tolerate people is deeply compromised and requiring them to remain in intense contact increases stress, anxiety, and resistance. The situation is not unlike weight training where intense, continuous activity can be counterproductive. The key to maximizing progress is a careful balance between the work periods that foster new skills and rest periods that permit recovery.

That's why the Spectacular Bond program is set up to ensure that periods of demanding activity are steadily intermixed with periods of rest and recovery. As this balance becomes a stable component of the children's lives, it transforms their view of the world. Instead of a place to fear and avoid, it becomes a place that is manageable and ultimately attractive.

The social contexts outlined in Chapter 4 are central to achieving this goal: Adult-led Exchange (ALE), Minimal Exchange (ME), No Exchange (NE), and Child-led Exchange (CLE).

- First, they enable the child to see the world as a place composed of clearly identifiable contexts.

- Second, each of the contexts presents varying demands, so the child learns how to function in a range of settings. The child learns to deal effectively with the major situations encountered in daily life.

- Third, the child learns that demanding activities are limited in time and are balanced by periods of relaxation.

Organizing the day according to social contexts

(1) Adult-Led Exchange (ALE)

Adult-led exchanges are those encounters during the day when you are guiding the child's behavior—generally to build particular skills or facilitate certain activities. Quiet sitting is one example of ALE. Other such exchanges occur throughout the course of the day, primarily in the routines of everyday life, such as meals, snack time, bath time, and getting dressed.

GUIDELINE 1: SCHEDULING SHORT, REGULAR PERIODS OF ADULT-LED EXCHANGE (ALE)

Schedule one period of ALE with your child approximately every hour. The interaction should last about five to ten minutes, though for meals it can last longer (up to 20 minutes). Over the course of a day, aim for about eight to ten ALE periods. This arrangement means that

- your child cannot tune out for extended periods of time and

- the interaction is brief enough to avoid your child feeling overwhelmed.

This exemplifies the balance between involvement and rest that the program strives for.

A typical set of ALEs might look like this:

Time	Activity
8:00-8:20 AM	Breakfast
9:00-9:15 AM	Child gets dressed and brushes teeth
10:00-10:15 AM	Quiet sitting (duration will depend on how far along you are in this activity)

11:00-11:30 AM	Walk to the park
12:30-12:50 PM	Lunch
2:00-2:15 PM	Quiet sitting
3:30-3:45 PM	Snack
5:30-5:45 PM	Bath
6:30-6:50 PM	Dinner
8:00 PM	Child brushes teeth

At any point during an ALE, you should be prepared to deal with disruptive behaviors that the child might show (e.g., getting up from the table, throwing toys out of the bath, and so on). This is particularly true at the start of the program when the child is still adapting to the new routines. Follow the guidelines in Chapters 6 and 7 for handling these behaviors.

For a child who attends school, the hours before and after school should be arranged to allow for these interaction periods. Because less time is available, there may be fewer periods.

GUIDELINE 2: USING SHORT, SIMPLE COMMANDS TO CARRY OUT ADULT-LED EXCHANGE

Ensure that each ALE period is carefully paced and well structured. You will find that the use of short, simple commands (described in Chapter 5) will help you reach that goal. You state in tiny step-by-step detail exactly what the child has to do, and you pause at each step to make sure it is carried out before you move on. It is as if life is conducted in slow motion with everything on hold until a command is followed. For example, mealtime can be marked by instructions such as the following: "Please stand up," "Walk to the table," "Sit down on this chair," "Take the spoon," and so on.

Examples of Short, Simple Commands for ALE

Bath time

"Go to the bathroom." (With your hands on your child's shoulders, walk with your child to the bathroom.)

"Take this arm out." (Point to arm and help child remove one arm from shirt.)

"Take out the other one." (Point to arm and help child remove other arm from shirt.)

"Lift this leg." (Help child remove one leg from pants.)

"Lift that leg." (Help child remove other leg from pants.)

"Take off your underwear." (Assist child as needed.)

"Get in the tub." (Assist child as needed.)

Getting dressed

"Take this shirt." (Hand child the shirt.)

"Put your hand in the sleeve." (Assist child as needed.)

"Put your other hand in the sleeve." (Assist child as needed.)

"Put this leg in the pants." (Assist child as needed.)

"Put that leg in the pants." (Assist child as needed.)

Going for a walk

"Pick up these shoes."

"Sit down here." (Point to chair.)

"Put your foot in the shoe." (Assist child as needed.)

"Put that foot in the shoe." (Assist child as needed.)

"Pick up this coat." (Point to coat.)

"Put your arm in the sleeve." (Assist child as needed.)

"Put that arm in the sleeve." (Assist child as needed.)

Children on the spectrum crave sameness. The routines of daily life are ideal for meeting this need. At the same time, you are going to transform these activities so that they are carried out in a much more controlled and careful manner. This requires that the child focus more attention on you. In essence, you are using the known world of routines to get the child comfortable with the unknown world of interaction.

In putting the above practices in place, your message to the child is that you are committed to guiding the behavior, but you will never do it in a way that is overpowering or unbearable. You want your child to have the feeling that new demands are ones that never exceed his or her capabilities. *The importance of this message cannot be overstated. It is the foundation upon which the child can build a base of trust in key human relationships.*

GUIDELINE 3: AVOIDING QUESTIONS

In keeping with the principle of simplification, questions are avoided in ALE. As we mentioned earlier, parents often respond to this guideline by asking "Does that mean I don't talk to my child?" The answer is "Of course, not." Instead, speak to your child via comments. For example, while out on a walk, you might make observations such as, "That is such a pretty bird. It is so good at flying," or "Wow, lots of children are in the park today. But still there's room on the swings. We can go on the swings." In other words, when the child is calm, you can say quite a lot without asking any questions.

GUIDELINE 4: RESPONDING TO THE CHILD'S REQUESTS BY SAYING "NOT NOW"

One of the components in ALE that parents find unnerving is the handling of the child's requests for desires (for a toy, for an activity, and so forth). Consistent with the framework offered in Chapter 7, the most effective way to respond is to say, "Not now."

You may still have doubts about taking this approach since it seems so counterintuitive. Should that be the case, it's best to take a few minutes and reread Chapter 7.

GUIDELINE 5: LIMITING DISPLAYS OF AFFECTION

Displays of affection play an important role in life and in the program. However, aside from some set, short routines (such as kissing your child upon his or her return from school), displays of affection do not take place during ALE. As you will see, they play a major role in another context: child-led exchange (CLE).

GUIDELINE 6: HOLDING OFF ON OTHER ACTIVITIES (LIKE TEACHING AND INTERACTIVE PLAYING)

Teaching sessions and interactive play sessions are common forms of ALE and they are going to play an increasingly important role as your child advances. However, in the early phases they are not part of the program. The reason? The children have not yet mastered the patterns of interaction needed to be successful learners. As a result they are likely to resist full participation in any teaching. The practice of resistance is something to be avoided when at all possible.

(2) Minimal Exchange Period (MEP)

The next social context, the Minimal Exchange Period (MEP), is one that occurs when the adult and child are together but are not engaged in any interaction. Children on the spectrum often have difficulty finding things to do when left to their own devices. This has been described by parents in the following ways:

> "Adam has no way of occupying himself. He wants my attention all the time."

"Taking Derek to a restaurant is unbearable—until the food comes, he gets up and wanders around."

"When we were at the bank, Melissa jumped away from me and pulled all the forms off the counter and made a mess."

Though the statements vary, they share a common core. They reflect the difficulties the children experience when no one is guiding their behavior and occupying their time.

The goal of MEP is to broaden the children's repertoire of social behavior so that, even when there is no attention from others, they are comfortable and can occupy themselves with appropriate activities. Self-control in the presence of others is a vital skill, and with its attainment the children are able to cope effectively with a much wider variety of daily life encounters.

To practice this skill, it's best if you determine a period of time each day when you and your child can be together in the same room, with no interaction taking place. You can be sitting reading a newspaper, writing out a grocery list, or daydreaming—but do not be on your phone or computer. The message is that you are there and present, but aside from an emergency, you are not available to provide guidance or direction. Your child may entertain himself or herself with games, books, or toys, or he or she may choose to do nothing.

GUIDELINE 7: SELECTING THE PLACE

Any room of the house that is a confined space with a door can be used, but it should not be your child's room. If you wish, different rooms of the house may be used on different days (e.g., one day, it could be the kitchen while you are cooking; another day it could be the den while you are reading a book, and so on).

GUIDELINE 8: PROVIDING MATERIALS

The room should contain some toys or games (10 or fewer) that are appropriate for your child and set out in places that the child can access without your help. There should be no electronic devices available—the child cannot use this time to watch TV, play computer games, or use the iPad. When these devices are available, children escape into them and lose contact with the real world. If a computer or TV are in the room, they should simply be kept off.

GUIDELINE 9: SETTING THE TIME

MEP should take place when your child is well rested and not tired. Aim for periods of about 20 to 30 minutes, although at the outset, they may be shorter.

GUIDELINE 10: FRAMING THE INTERACTION

Take your child's hand and say, "Come with me." Once in the room, you will begin your own activity (such as those listed above). Your child does not have to use the toys or other materials in the room, and you should not try to get your child to use them. Do not say things like, "Oh look the Legos are there. Why don't you play with them?"

You will need a few sessions before your child understands what is expected. During that time you may find the following helpful in dealing with issues that arise:

How to handle stims

The new context is likely to elicit some stimming. Brief periods of stimming that last less than a minute should be ignored. However, sustained periods should be handled using the techniques described in Chapter 6. Early on, it can be helpful to end MEP once your child has successfully resisted stimming for a certain period of time (refer to the guidelines in Chapter 6). The end result is a win for both participants. You have achieved your point and your child sees that your demands are manageable.

How to handle aimless behavior

Another pattern that may emerge is for the child to wander around, touching various items and objects in an aimless manner. An item may be picked up, dropped within a minute, followed by moving on to the next, and so on.

One of the goals of MEP is to facilitate your child achieving more organized behavior. You can help this happen by removing items or placing them out of reach if you know that they will elicit disorganized or unthinking patterns of behavior (e.g., strings on window shades). However, do not attempt to remove all of the material, even if you can. The child needs to learn that objects in reach are not always available for handling. These include paper covers on books, pillows, pencils and the like.

While you will appear to be relaxed with your mind occupied elsewhere, you are actually watching your child carefully. Since you know your child well, you almost certainly know when these behaviors are likely to start. As soon as you see hints that they are emerging, position yourself to prevent them from happening. The principles for doing so are the same as those for handling repetitive behaviors (described in Chapter 6).

How to handle your child's attempts at interaction

Many children try to get their parents involved while in MEP, generally by making requests. If the child requests a desire (something that is not essential), just shrug your shoulders and say nothing. This conveys the message that you heard the request, but do not intend to act on it.

If the child requests a need (something that is essential such as using the bathroom), help him or her in whatever ways are needed, but try to say as little as possible. If the bathroom requests are repeated (in an effort to gain your involvement), simply shrug and say nothing.

If the child starts to climb on you in an effort to sit on your lap and start cuddling, position yourself to prevent the action—for example, you might stand up and move away. This is similar to the avoidance of affection in ALE, and it is done for the same reason. The goal of the exchange is to enable the child to accept self-regulation of behavior and this cannot be achieved if he or she is using affection to control the exchange and engage you.

In combination, these various actions convey the message that you are there and will help with essential needs. Aside from that, the child begins to realize that he or she can manage independently without the guidance of others.

(3) No Exchange Period (NEP)

Almost all parents, frustrated by their child's behavior, have said at one time or another, "Go to your room!" This setup frames the room as a form of punishment.

We view the child's room in a different light, and the program sets things up so as to convey this to the child as well. His or her room is the place where all the turmoil of daily life can be left outside the door. As such, it offers the children an assured place of calm and respite that they can always rely on.

There are many advantages to using the child's room as a respite center. It is a space that the children know well. It is a space that contains the toys and possessions they like. It is a place that is devoid of people. Psychologically, it has the potential to be as far removed from punishment as any situation could possibly be. Using the child's room as a haven enables them to see that relief is never far away.

In the beginning the children do not know this—particularly if the room has been used for time-outs and punishment in the past. As with all parts of the program, however, if this component is put in place in a calm, consistent manner, the children generally make the transition within one to two weeks. Parents often comment, with surprise, "I never thought it would happen, but he really loves being in his room now."

Alone time yields amazing benefits. But it's essential that the room be totally safe. Make sure to check out the many resources on websites and in books that outline ways to childproof the home. If you want to keep a steady eye on what is happening, install a safety gate so that the child stays in the room but you can still observe everything that is going on.

GUIDELINE 11: SELECTING THE ROOM

Parents often ask if the child's room is the only place that can be used for respite. It is generally the best place, but at times that isn't possible (such as when the room is shared with a sibling or when it does not have a solid door). In these situations other rooms can be used. Whatever place is selected should have the following characteristics:

- It should be a confined area with a door that can be closed if needed.

- No other person should be in the room when the child is there for rest and relaxation.

- It should be available throughout the day so that it can be used at any time that you choose.

GUIDELINE 12: PREPARING THE ROOM

The room should contain a small number of toys and other materials your child likes (10 to 12 objects). It is also useful to set things up so that the toys can be placed in boxes and easily moved in and out when necessary.

It's great if music is available that the child can play on a CD player or iPod. Other than that, there should be no high-tech devices such as computers, TVs, and handheld games. If they are in the room, disconnect them or take them out.

If there are pieces of furniture in the room that your child attempts to disassemble, such as dresser drawers, it's best to remove them. You are not asking the child to do particular activities in the room, but at the same time you do not want to give him or her the opportunity to carry out counterproductive activities.

The arrangement presents the children with three choices:

- they can do nothing,

- they can engage in repetitive behaviors, or

- they can play productively.

The last option is, of course, wonderful. However, the other two are fine as well. The room is "their time." It's okay if they choose to stim. Many people on the spectrum report how stimming helps them manage and lessen their anxiety. The children may have times when they need to stim, and their room is an excellent place for them to engage—solo—in these activities.

GUIDELINE 13: CHOOSING THE TIME

Even though the room is the child's domain, the decision as to when to use the room is yours. Overall, you should aim to use it once or twice a day. A good time to use the room is after a significant encounter has taken place, such as quiet sitting or a controlled exchange.

When a child has been working hard and is tired, a period in the room is ideal. Parents know their children well, so if you sense that your child is fatigued by an encounter, it's wise to be proactive and use the room to head off or prevent a meltdown.

You can also use the room to make your life run a bit smoother. For example, if you have an important phone call, have your child stay in the room during this time.

Once you have decided to initiate a No Exchange Period, say to your child, "Go to your room for a while," and then guide him or her there if needed. Once your child is in the room, close the door. At the beginning when things are not yet clear to your child, he or she may try to get out. Simply hold the door closed from the outside and say nothing. If you talk, your child senses that the issue is open for negotiation. In general, while a child is crying or shouting, do not open the door. On the other hand, if at least five minutes has passed, and the child has quieted down, you can open the door and say, "Now you can come out."

When you do this, you may be surprised at what follows. When the children are allowed to leave, they sometimes elect to stay in the room. This is fine because it helps them to feel in control—and you have not said anything to the contrary. Continue standing there with the door open, and when your child is ready, he or she will choose to exit. A situation like this presents the children with an opportunity where it's perfectly fine for them to decide what to do. (See the section *Some Other Contexts* below.)

That's why when you open the door, you do not say, "Leave your room." Instead, your phrasing offers an option ("You can come out"). In the rare instance that your child might remain in the room for a sustained period of 20 minutes or more, simply go in and guide the child out.

GUIDELINE 14: ALLOWING YOUR CHILD TO CHOOSE WHEN TO USE THE ROOM (WITH SOME LIMITS)

The times outlined above were set at your discretion. You may find that your child elects to use the room as well at various points in the day. This is fine, and suggests that your child is experiencing the room as a pleasant place to be.

However, some children want to escape the world for longer periods than is desirable. In general, you should not allow your child to elect to use the room more than four times a day, with a maximum time of fifteen minutes each.

Should you find that your child is electing to stay in his or her room for long periods of the day or repeatedly throughout the day, then minimize the pattern. When you see your child heading in that direction, do not ask a question "Are you going to your room?" Instead, just stop your child and say, "Not now."

(4) Child-led Exchange (CLE)

Child-led Exchange is the social context in which the child takes control and guides the adult. It is the time of day when you and your child can have a totally conflict-free, relaxed, and loving exchange that is fulfilling for both of you.

GUIDELINE 15: SELECTING THE TIME AND PLACE

CLE takes place at the end of the day when the child is still reasonably alert yet able to relax. The child's room is the best place, but any other quiet, contained area is acceptable. The length of time should be about 30 minutes.

After the main evening routine (dinner, brushing teeth, etc.), go with your child to the room. Only the child and one or both parents should be in the room during this period. In general, siblings should not be included, though you may want to create a similar period for each of your other children.

GUIDELINE 16: ALLOWING A RANGE OF ACTIVITIES

During CLE your child chooses what to do and how to interact with you. Some activities that children choose during this period are

Hugging, kissing, and cuddling with parents
Playing games
Looking at books together
Singing songs
Jumping on the bed
Rolling on the floor

The prohibited activities are few but involve
Electronic devices
Self-injurious behaviors
Destructive or aggressive behaviors

GUIDELINE 17: ALLOWING YOUR CHILD TO BE IN CHARGE

The person in charge of CLE is your child. If he or she for whatever reason chooses to do nothing, that is entirely acceptable. Do not try to engage your child with comments such as, "Wouldn't you like to play a game?" "Look at this nice book," or "Do you want to jump on the bed?" The child can do any and all of those, but only if he or she initiates them without any prompting.

In other words you do not suggest, instruct, hint or otherwise try to get an activity going. The purpose of this time is to allow your child to guide you and to lead the interaction. This is your child's time to be in charge, and you should simply follow his or her lead.

Many parents describe this period of the day as heaven. Some families refer to this period as "Loving Time" because they are free to show each other affection. This is a wonderful way to spend the time, but it's important to remember that your child gets to decide whether or not to be affectionate with you, not the other way around.

Some Other Contexts

The contexts we've been discussing cover most of the child's experiences in the home. There are some others that we have not discussed such as playing with siblings in the back yard, observing other children playing, taking a ride in the car, and others. These form part of the background of the child's life and they do not require much attention or effort on your part.

The times you may have to get involved are when your child engages in some destructive behaviors. Generally, it's best if you get the child out of the setting and back to the house. If the behavior is in a car, you need to ignore it and try to get to your destination as quickly and safely as possible. Resist the urge to give your child commands when you are driving the car if the child is not likely to comply.

Don't be concerned if things fail to go well during one or two of these periods. They are not the dominant part of the child's day. The most important message you can send to your child is that you are calm and controlled even when things are a bit out of line. As best as you can, try to be observant and learn your child's patterns so that you can think ahead to prevent difficulties from arising in the future. This might mean avoiding, for the time being, long car rides or other contexts where your child's behavior is likely to deteriorate.

Putting It All Together: Overview of the Day

Below are sample schedules that incorporate all the social contexts described in this chapter. Use it as a guide, remembering to create a schedule that works best for you. For example, if your child is having various therapy sessions, such as occupational therapy or physical therapy, adjust the day accordingly.

Sample schedule for days when the child does not attend school

Time	Type of exchange	Activity
8:00-8:10 AM	ALE	Child gets dressed and brushes teeth
8:30-8:50 AM	ALE	Breakfast
9:00-9:45 AM	other context	Child plays alone or with siblings in house
9:45-10:30 AM	ALE	Quiet sitting
10:30-10:50 AM	NEP	Child relaxes in room
11:00-11:10 AM	ALE	Walk to the park
11:10-11:45 AM	other context	Play at the park and then walk home

12:00-12:20 PM	ALE	Lunch
12:45-1:15 PM	MEP	Child and parent in room together
1:15-2:00 PM	other context	Child plays alone or with siblings in the house
2:00-2:45 PM	ALE	Quiet sitting
3:00-3:20 PM	NEP	Child relaxes in room
3:30-3:45 PM	ALE	Snack
3:45-4:45 PM	other context	Child plays alone or with siblings outside
4:45-5:00 PM	ALE	Bath
5:00-5:30 PM	other context	Child watches TV
5:40-6:00 PM	ALE	Dinner
6:00-6:30 PM	other context	Child plays games on iPad
6:30-6:45 PM	ALE	Child brushes teeth
7:00-7:30 PM	CLE	Period of Child-led Exchange
8:00 PM		Bedtime

Sample schedule for days when the child attends school

Time	Type of exchange	Activity
8:00-8:30 AM	ALE	Child gets dressed, brushes teeth, and has breakfast
SCHOOL		
2:00-2:20 PM	NEP	Child relaxes in room
2:30-3:15 PM	ALE	Quiet sitting
3:15-3:30 PM	other context	Play time in back yard
3:30-3:45 PM	ALE	Snack
3:45-4:15 PM	MEP	Period of Minimal Exchange
4:15-4:45 PM	other context	Play time in family room
4:45-5:00 PM	ALE	Walk to the park
5:00-5:30 PM	other context	Play at park and walk home
5:40-6:00 PM	ALE	Dinner
6:00-6:30 PM	other context	Child plays games on iPad
6:30-6:45 PM	ALE	Child brushes teeth
7:00-7:30 PM	CLE	Period of Child-led Exchange
8:00 PM		Bedtime

At the outset of the program, a significant part of the day may be occupied by the controlled exchanges outlined in Chapter 6 since you will be putting these in place and the child may engage in long periods of resistance. This means that less time will be available for the contexts described above. That is to be expected, and is not a source of concern. The daily schedule will change from day to day and week to week. Over time, as the child gets comfortable with the new patterns you have put in place, more time will be available for other activities.

. . . .

FREQUENTLY ASKED QUESTIONS:

What are other examples of activities that can be done during the periods of Adult-Led Exchange (ALE)?

Simple everyday routines provide ample opportunity for ALE. Eating meals and snacks, getting dressed and undressed, brushing teeth, taking a bath, getting ready to go outside for a walk, and so on. As these simple routines improve and become easy for your child to do in a calm, deliberate manner, you can begin to expand the interactions to include other easy-to-do activities, such as helping take laundry from the dryer or helping clear items from the kitchen table.

During mealtime, my child stands on the chair and laughs. Sometimes she runs around the room. What do I do?

The goal is to have your child seated at the table for the entire meal. Inappropriate behavior should not be permitted. The techniques described in Chapter 6 are ideally suited for achieving the calm discipline that you are striving for.

Is the Minimal Exchange Period (MEP) optional or mandatory?

In the busy pattern of everyday life, it is easy to overlook this activity. On an occasional basis, that is fine. The schedule is not rigid and you do not need to do it everyday, but you should ensure that it happens four to five times a week. The benefits can be considerable. It lays the groundwork for the child being able to cope with a wide variety of situations where he or she has to tolerate not being engaged (such as waiting in a restaurant or doctor's office).

Can I talk on the phone during Minimal Exchange Period (MEP)?

The brief answer is no—but the real answer is a bit more complicated. Rather than talking to someone on the phone, it is extremely useful for you to pretend to be talking to someone on the phone. That way, without upsetting the non-existent person on the other end, you can quickly put the phone aside when you see that your child is exhibiting undesirable behaviors. This sends the message that you are always alert, even when you are on the phone. This lays the groundwork for you to eventually be able to talk on the phone without any disturbance when your child is with you.

Can other people be in the room with us during the Minimal Exchange Period (MEP)?

At the beginning others should not be present. After a few weeks, if there are family members who are comfortable with what you are doing and will not interfere, they can be present as well. All people in the room must be sending the same consistent message: "This is a time when we are together, but we are not available to interact with you."

As the child gains self-control, you can bring other people such as friends and family into the setting. Interact with them as if you are in a typical social encounter, such as having someone over for coffee. If the child reverts to an undesirable behavior, immediately stop the conversation and turn your full attention to your child. That tells the child that, despite appearances to the contrary, you are ever alert to his or her behaviors. That message is powerful. It says that attempts to engage in unproductive behaviors will not be successful. Over time, your child will begin to show self-control regardless of whether you are alone or occupied with someone else.

Can I use the playroom or family room for the No Exchange Period (NEP)?

It's best to select a room with a door that can be closed, has only a limited number of toys, is childproof, and can ensure privacy for the child without others moving in and out. If the playroom and family room meet these requirements, they can be used for NEP. If they do not, they should not be used for NEP.

10

Moving On

Element 6

The sixth element of the program adds a new facet to the bond you are creating with your child. The first five elements have a common focus aimed at fostering "calm control." Your goal has been to help the child "turn off" counterproductive behaviors such as stims and tantrums.

The sixth element is different. It is aimed at "turning on" particular behaviors, specifically the ones that lay the foundation for effective learning. Put in the language of neurology, with *inhibition* established, we are going to be adding *activation*. Using simple actions that require little effort or exertion, you are going to be teaching your child to follow a series of commands under your direction.

This element should only be started after the other five elements are well established and have been running smoothly for two weeks. Most children are ready to begin this element about eight to twelve weeks into the program. While the sixth element is introduced, it is important to continue the previous five elements.

"Turning off" versus "Turning on"

"Turning off" and "turning on" may be unfamiliar terms, but your experience in school and in your child's intervention programs has almost certainly made you familiar with the "turning on" approach.

"Turning on" is the basis for almost all work done with children on the spectrum. It's why, from the outset, many programs try to get the children to recognize and name colors, letters, shapes and the like. The focus is on having the children do what they have not been doing. But because this is instituted before self-control has been attained, the teaching sessions are repeatedly interrupted by a host of uncontrolled behaviors, such as stims and meltdowns, that interfere with learning.

This push for turning on new skills is completely understandable, but it overlooks a basic fact. As reflected in the old saying, "You can lead a horse to water, but you can't make it drink," it can be difficult to get someone, especially a young child, to produce an action that you want. That's why hundreds of hours are often spent in getting them to do what seem to be super-simple behaviors. The time is needed—not because the children are incapable—but because they are bringing in the protective (avoidance) mechanisms they possess to keep the adult at bay.

In contrast to the difficulties of making someone "do," it is relatively easy to have someone "not do." If we continue the horse analogy and assume, for example, that we do not want the horse to drink, there are several options that can succeed, such as covering the water, removing the water, positioning the horse so he cannot drink, and other possibilities. The issue here is simply recognizing the reality that "not doing" is easier to achieve than "doing."

In the case of children with ASD, the benefits of teaching inhibition prior to teaching activation are immense and go far beyond ease of execution. Inhibition serves as a stepping stone to activation. Interactions focused on teaching inhibition provide the child with two clear messages:

- an adult can control the child's behavior, and

- this can be done without overwhelming the child's resources.

Excessive pressure on the child to "do" a new task, such as answer a question or learn a new concept, are out of the picture. At the same time the child is required to attend to the adult and to follow some basic guidelines. This presents the child with a much safer social world.

Once "not doing" is firmly in place, "doing" becomes a feasible and desirable goal. That is where we are headed now.

Imitating Simple Actions

The "doing" activities introduced here are extremely easy to carry out. The child watches you do a simple action, such as hugging a toy, and he or she then will imitate that action. Because the actions are so undemanding, they may strike you as requiring the child to do very little. *That's exactly what we would like the child to feel as well.*

Children with ASD experience transitions (e.g., a new activity) and intrusions (e.g., demands from adults) to be extremely taxing. By keeping the early activities as simple as possible, we are helping to lower the anxiety and resistance that can so readily appear. The arrangement also sends an important message that the child can trust you to demand only what is within his or her capabilities.

Despite their apparent simplicity, the activities are designed to achieve a significant goal. You are showing the child that from this point forward there is a new understanding in place:

- you will be introducing new, unpredictable information—but in carefully managed ways,

- the child is expected to follow your lead, and

- you are equipped to ensure that the child follows through with what you have requested.

The key features of the simple actions are:

- They do not require the children to process or produce language; they require only that they observe and imitate your actions. At the outset, this route is more powerful than language in establishing effective interaction.

- They are completed over a short period of about 3 to 5 minutes.

- They involve real-life objects and actions. This allows the exercises to readily be inserted throughout the day, thereby encouraging generalization to daily life.

- They are done only when the adult has the time and ability to ensure that the child complies and when the child is in a relatively receptive state (e.g., not hungry, not tired, and not upset).

GUIDELINE 1: SELECTING THE TIME AND PLACE

The actions can be carried out in any room of the house (excluding the child's room, which should be kept as a haven). It's helpful to vary the location occasionally so that the child does not get the mind-set that "doing" occurs in only one location.

The actions can be carried out any time of the day as long as the child is alert and it is not close to bedtime. It is good to do a session at least once a day; it is even better to do it twice a day—with at least a half hour between the sessions.

GUIDELINE 2: ARRANGING THE OBJECTS

Identify some common, unbreakable objects in your home. These might include spoons, pens, plastic cups, wastepaper baskets, small toys, a pad of note paper, or a book. In other words, select simple familiar objects that usually attract little notice or interest. Try to choose at least 20 different objects. In any single session you will use 8 to 10 of them.

In preparation for the activity, place each item in a different location in the room. The items should not be grouped into a cluster. Placing the items in different locations fosters greater generalization by sending the child the message that directives to do things can occur at any time and in any place.

Different objects should be used from one session to the next so that the child does not link the activity to a particular set of objects. After the session, the objects should be removed and they should not be available for the child to play with.

GUIDELINE 3: CARRYING OUT THE SIMPLE ACTIONS

The simple actions that you and your child will perform all involve an object. Below is a list of actions followed by a description of how each action should be performed.

- Shake—shake the object back and forth a few times, and then put it down.

- Hug—bring the object to your chest and bring your other hand to your chest so that both hands are covering the object, then put the object down.

- Turn over—pick up the object, turn it over, and put it back down.

- Point to—hold your index finger out and touch the object with the tip of your finger. (If your child has difficulty with pointing, you can modify the action to full hand extension where the whole hand touches the object.)

- Tap— pick up the object, tap it against the work surface (usually a table), and put it back down.

- Drop in—drop the object in a basket or drawer.

- Take out—take an object from inside a basket or drawer.

- Pull—move the object along the surface toward you. (It is preferable not to use toy vehicles for this action since vehicles "call for" the pulling action.)

- Push—move the object along the work surface away from you.

All the actions are ones that can be carried out on any object. In other words, in contrast to "rolling a car" or "flying a plane," the actions are not ones that are tied to any object. This leads, at times, to some rather strange behaviors such as hugging a bus. However, the key criterion is not familiarity. Rather it is a clearly discernible action that the child can recognize and easily carry out. All the actions above meet these criteria.

At the start of the activity, both you and your child stand or sit near the object. Hold your child close to you by putting your arm around his or her waist. This keeps the child in your "space," thereby leading the child to attend more carefully to you and to realize that you are guiding the exchange. Ensure that your position is comfortable and stable, so that if your child makes an effort to run away or throw the object you are well positioned to stop this from happening.

With your free arm, take the object and carry out the action that you plan (e.g., pick up the spoon, tap it on the table, and put it down). At the same time, give the simple instruction, "Do this." You then wait until the child executes the action. But waiting, particularly at the outset, is not sufficient. From past experience, you know that it is likely that the child will tune you out or try and engage in some other activity. Those alternative routes can be closed off by the simple action of supporting the child's hand.

GUIDELINE 4: SUPPORTING THE CHILD'S HAND

If you position yourself so that you are holding the child's preferred hand (e.g., the right hand if the child is right-handed), you will find that the child is far more likely to execute the requested movement. While you are holding one arm around your child's waist, use your other hand to hold the child's preferred hand near the object. Then wait for the child to make the appropriate movement. We refer to this technique as *hand support*. In hand support you are holding the child's hand, but you are *not* moving it.

If the child complies easily and does the correct movement without any resistance, you do not need to maintain the hold for the rest of the exercises. The purpose of physically holding the child is to ensure that efforts to run away, throw objects, or otherwise disrupt the exercise will not be successful. Once the child is complying easily and accurately, there is no need to hold the child. Just model the action and wait until your child imitates it.

Hand support is often essential in the early stages. As we said before, this technique involves holding the child's hand without moving it. It is qualitatively different from "hand-over-hand" modeling where the adult actively moves the child's hand. An observer may not be able to tell the difference, but as the one providing the hand contact, you will know the difference because you can feel what is happening.

Hand support is also amazingly helpful for the many children who have difficulty with motor control. As Ido Kedar, a young man with autism writes,

> It helps many autistic people to have someone touch or even support their arm.... This is due to our trouble initiating [motor actions] and getting our bodies to obey our minds. This slight touch seems to help unlock the sort of paralysis I have described.
>
> (*Ido in Autismland*)

This does not mean that the hand-over-hand technique is never used. In the early stages you may need to model the movement using the hand-over-hand technique if the child doesn't seem to understand what you expect him or her to do or the child seems frozen in inactivity.

The exercise is not considered complete, however, until the child does the movement independently. An independent movement is one where the child initiates and completes the movement without you *guiding* his or her hand. In independent movement, you can still be providing hand support when necessary.

GUIDELINE 5: SELECTING THE NUMBER AND CONTENT OF THE ACTION SEQUENCES

One session should include eight to ten actions.

Sample session (these are only suggestions—the actual details can, and should, vary from the list below):

	Object	Location	Action	Description
1	Spoon	Dining table	Shake	Pick up the spoon, shake it back and forth a few times, and then put it down
2	Plastic cup	Chair	Hug	Pick up the cup, bring it to your chest and bring your other hand to your chest as well, then put the cup down
3	Note pad	Coffee table	Turn Over	Pick up the note pad, flip it over, and put it back down
4	Ball	Floor	Point to	Hold your index finger out and touch the ball with the tip of your finger
5	Marker	Desk	Tap	Pick up the marker, then tap it against the desk, and put it back down on the desk

6	Tissue	Laundry bin	Drop in	Pick up the tissue and drop it in the laundry bin
7	Remote control	Open drawer	Take out	Reach inside the drawer and pick up the remote control
8	Paper clip	Side table	Pull	Move the paper clip along the surface of the table toward you
9	Pencil	Chair	Push	Move the pencil along the seat of the chair away from you
10	Rubber band	Sofa	Hug	Pick up the rubber band, bring it to your chest and bring your other hand to your chest as well, then put the rubber band down

As indicated above, the same action is not repeated over and over. Rather the actions steadily vary from one request to the next. For example, if your first request involved pointing to one object, the next one might involve turning over a different object while the third request might involve dropping still another object. In other words, change is the name of the game.

This high level of variation within a super simple context is helpful in developing flexibility. When things are going smoothly, a session may last only a few minutes. To encourage flexibility, each session should be different from the previous one—both the objects and the actions should be changed.

GUIDELINE 6: HANDLING DIFFICULTIES

Many children find this activity appealing and readily adapt to its demands. It fits their desire to move and act upon objects. Some children, however, show a different reaction. These children are generally ones who are extremely sensitive to change and tend to be very reticent. Once a change is perceived, they resist it.

The children generally display their resistance by trying to move away from you, acting as though you are not present, or throwing the object. Difficulties of this sort can be overcome by securely holding the child close to you. This removes the option of a range of actions, such as running away or doing something else with the object. Instead, it once again places the children in a simple two choice situation: either they do what you request or they do nothing and wait. Given those options, they almost always prefer to do what you request.

Sometimes the resistance appears in a slightly different pattern. The child completes, in a sort of detached manner, the first couple of requests. Then apparently realizing that the requests are not a "one off" situation, but rather are going to continue, resistance sets in. Should this occur, don't be surprised or dismayed. You are becoming more observant as to what your child is doing and the patterns he or she is displaying. This is a major step in being able to help your child reach higher levels.

Regardless of the source, the difficulties are handled in the same way. Stay with your child and remain calm, cool, and silent. Just wait. Do not cajole, do not talk, and do not indicate impatience. Act as though you have all the time in the world, and it is of no concern to you if the wait is seemingly interminable. Continue to wait until the child completes the action appropriately.

Should the resistance last five minutes or more, do not aim to carry out a full session. Simply end the session once the child successfully completes your last request. As in all the interactions in the program, the message you want to send to your child is that compliance pays off. This means that at the beginning, your sessions may contain only one or two exercises.

We know how difficult it can be to follow the advice just offered. Intervention work has typically shown a lack of appreciation for quiet waiting. Yet, its power is enormous. It tells the child that you are not in the least bit anxious and you have every confidence that your goal will be achieved. It does mean, however, that the initial sessions require you to allocate a sustained period of time (generally up to half an hour) so that you can ensure success. Your message is this: "I have a few simple things for you to do, and I am prepared to wait as long as it takes until they are done." Experience will show you just how powerful that message can be.

GUIDELINE 7: TRANSFERRING TO OTHER SETTINGS

Activation demands lend themselves to a variety of settings where you can place one or two demands at any time of the day. For example,

- at dinner time you might turn over a spoon and request your child to do the same;

- in the bath, you might put a bar of soap in the water, retrieve it and ask your child to do the same;

- while dressing, you might point to a piece of clothing that the child is going to wear and ask your child to do the same.

As long as the action is clear and easily executed, you can ask it of your child. In all cases, spoken language remains minimal and restricted to the phrases, "do this" or "do that." In contrast to a "session," these out-of-session requests are limited to one or two commands and do not involve a sustained sequence of commands.

. . . .

FREQUENTLY ASKED QUESTIONS:

My child can do all the actions that you are using. Can I give something more challenging?

Not at this time. The aim is not to present your child with a new challenging activity, but rather to teach your child to "do" under the guidance of an adult. This is the foundation of all teaching. By minimizing the complexity of the action, we maximize the attention to the person. This is invaluable for the more advanced teaching that will follow.

Why is it important to hold the child?

The focus is not on the activities but on the relationship. By bringing the child into your space while completing some clear simple activities, the child begins to learn that interpersonal relationships are not as difficult as they thought. In many cases, once the children are comfortable, they begin to extend their interpersonal skills independently, even in the absence of specific instruction.

I understand that it's important for my child to learn both inhibition ("not doing") and activation ("doing"),

but why is so much of the program aimed at inhibition and only a small section on activation?

In our experience most children on the spectrum have great problems with inhibition. They show limited ability to control their thoughts and actions, pace themselves, and reflect. Creating a foundation of self-control is the focus of this phase of the program. Once this foundation is created, the range and variety of skills the children can learn is phenomenal. By contrast, "doing" activities are much easier to attain. That last statement might conflict with your experience. But for the most part, "doing" activities prove to be difficult because the appropriate internal controls were not first set in place. With "not doing" and "simple doing" firmly in place, higher-level learning in language and other realms proceeds much faster and with greater effectiveness.

PART 3

Entering the Wider World

11

Stepping Out

What do I do at the supermarket? I dread going there. I never know how she'll handle it.

— Mother of Sheila, five-year-old with ASD

P arents often ask us at the start of the program how to handle routine errands outside the home. The answer is that, for the first part of the program, you are going to try your best not to bring your child into those situations. The ultimate goal, of course, is to have your child become a successful participant in the wider world. But you will need to hold off for a period of time. That's why all the components of the program discussed until now have focused on what you will be doing at home.

There are many reasons for taking this approach. Unlike public places your home offers a host of advantages. For a start, there are no outsiders who can make you uncomfortable by watching (and perhaps judging) how you handle things. Free of that unnecessary pressure, you can concentrate on what you need to do. Your home also contains the child's room—a safe, reliable place that is available anytime you need it.

The goal, of course, is not to limit yourself to the home. It is just a starting point. Once things are stable, you can move the program to the outside world.

Usually it takes between eight to twelve weeks to reach this point. How will you know when your child is ready? It's difficult to describe in words, but it will be apparent to you as you become more in tune with your child's body language. You will see a sense of calm in your child's eyes. You will see more modulated movements, and your child will seem generally more relaxed. You will find that your child is following your directions. This may not be present all day, every day, but it should become a significant part of your child's repertoire.

With that new base of behavior in place, you can begin to enter settings outside the home. Some children automatically transfer the controlled behavior to other settings. Many parents have told us that teachers report markedly improved behavior in school within a week or two of the program being implemented at home. Whether or not this happens for your child, the steps outlined in this chapter can ensure a successful transition of your child's new skills to the outside world. The key, as with all components of the program, is to plan ahead so you ensure the success that you are striving for.

GUIDELINE 1: IDENTIFYING SECURE SETTINGS AND THEN MAKING PLANS TO VISIT THEM

As noted above, outsiders are a common presence in the outside world and they can be, or can seem to be, judgmental. If a child is crying, for example, they may stare at you. So a first step in selecting places to apply the principles outside the home is to ensure that the places are ones where *you* feel comfortable and do not feel you are being judged.

This might be the house of a relative or neighbor who is sympathetic to what you are doing. It might be a shopping mall early on a Sunday morning when there are few people around. It might be a familiar neighborhood store, such as a pizza restaurant or an ice cream shop, with a friendly store manager. You can ask if there's a time of day when the store is likely to be empty, and then let them know what you'd like to do. The important point is to be in a place where you are able to implement the program in a manner similar to what you do at home without feeling tense.

In many ways these settings mirror the Minimal Exchange context that you employ at home. For example, if you are visiting a friend's house, you should act as if your focus is on the friend, but at the same time be vigilant about what the child is doing. At any sign of difficulty, you immediately turn your attention to the child and employ the same techniques you would use at home for the behavior that you see. All the techniques you employed at home to control troublesome behaviors are ones you can and should apply in these "comfortable" outside settings.

It can also be valuable to elicit negative behavior so that the child learns to control it in public places. For example, you can choose a setting in which your child is likely to want something that he or she cannot have, such as a particular item on a shelf. Once your child has made a request, respond with, "Not now." If a temper tantrum follows, handle it just as you would at home. When the encounter is over, it's best to head home or to a place where you and your child can relax, such as a familiar park.

GUIDELINE 2: LIMITING THE TIME

When you take your child outside the home, be careful not to exceed your child's capacity for self-control. For example, a 30-minute visit to a friend's house might fit the bill. At the beginning try to keep trips outside the house to less than 90 minutes, and have a plan in place to easily get back to the house should it be necessary. For example, if you anticipate that getting the child into a car might be difficult, do not go to a place that requires a car. Select a place closer to home.

GUIDELINE 3: SHOPPING

Grocery shopping is a regular activity where children often accompany their parents. Most children enjoy the experience, but still it needs to be handled carefully. It should not be introduced until your child has succeeded in showing control in simpler settings, such as a relative's home or a nearly empty restaurant.

A good way to introduce grocery shopping is to go to the market for an unnecessary trip. Select a time of day when the market is likely to be relatively free of people. Before entering the store, tell your child that you are planning to get one or two items (things that the child is familiar with). Then go into the store, select the items, go to the cashier, and check out. If your child is cooperating, he or she can be the one to select the items off the shelves.

The key is to keep the trip short so that the child's patience and level of tolerance are not challenged. If the child shows any negative response—even subtle ones, such as whining—put the items back and simply say, "We are going back home." Then immediately return home. You may get shouts and screams, but maintain your calm and do not threaten or punish. The message to the child is that counterproductive behavior does not pay off. Often, parents tell us that from that point on, the children handle the shopping with far greater ease.

As your child adapts to this situation, you can extend the shopping list and the time you spend at the store. But until you are certain that the behavior is stable, do not plan "real shopping"—that is, shopping where you are planning to buy needed items. For the first several weeks, you must always be ready to calmly leave the store and the items should your child start to misbehave.

GUIDELINE 4: ATTENDING RELIGIOUS SERVICES

For many families attendance at religious services is a treasured activity. Because of its structured, predictable nature, it can become a very appealing activity for the children as well. However, like all the activities it has to be carefully paced. Just as in the grocery store, this is not a setting where you want to apply your full range of techniques. If any troubles emerge, your plan is to exit quickly.

The best approach is to determine a time period that your child can tolerate and plan your visit to be a few minutes less. For example, if you feel that your child can handle a 15-minute period of self-control, plan your visit to be 10 minutes. That way you leave on a high note.

Select a seat that will make it easy for you to leave. Bring along a book, toy, or electronic device that your child likes. (The plan is to offer these only if absolutely necessary.) For example, you may have set a 10-minute goal, and your child is getting antsy at five minutes. You can then give the device to your child so that he or she is occupied for another few minutes. Do not allow lengthy periods of self-involved play. When your time limit is reached, take the device away and then leave.

Over the weeks plan to increase the time you spend there based on what you observe in your child. It is also useful to link your stay with the activities that your child enjoys. For example, if your child likes music, time your visit so it coincides with the music portion of the service.

GUIDELINE 5: THE MAGIC NUMBER "THREE"

In general, if you are able to execute your plans in three different outside settings (e.g., a friend's home, a store, and church), it transfers to all other settings. The child gets the message that this is an expected part of daily life and not a routine confined to the house. When this realization takes place, parents have reported a sense of freedom they thought had been lost forever. It's a phenomenal reward for all the work you have done.

A Final Note

It's hard to overstate the value of having your child see you in the outside world as someone who is totally calm and in charge. It sends the message, "Wherever we are, the same rules hold, and I will do whatever is needed to ensure that they are maintained." The children may offer some initial resistance, but it is generally short-lived. After a few carefully selected encounters, they not only accept the extension of self-control outside the home, they welcome it. The wider world is now "theirs" and they appreciate this expansion in their lives.

. . . .

FREQUENTLY ASKED QUESTIONS:

What do you suggest I do when strangers approach my child and start asking questions?

Strangers and the language they use can be major stressors for the child. It's important to protect your child from that stress. Remember that your interest is your child and not the stranger, so your goal is to end to the encounter. One way to do this is to say to the stranger in a calm, gentle tone, "My child has problems with language, and it's best not to ask questions." That will generally lead the stranger to end the interaction, which is what you want to happen.

There are also situations where your child is the initiator of the interaction. For example, he or she might approach a stranger and try to offer affection, such as a hug. That behavior, even when accepted by the stranger, is not appropriate, so once again your goal is to end the interaction.

It's generally best to intervene immediately by taking your child's hands and saying slowly, "Please stop." This is likely to lead your child to feel a bit uncomfortable. While the discomfort is not overwhelming, it can have powerful effects. It leads your child to think in comparable situations, "I had better not try hugging here because it can lead to that funny response from my mother." This internalization is critical to your child learning to control inappropriate behavior.

You said that the program initially is done only at home and that outside contexts should be discouraged. But she goes to school every day. How do we handle this?

Fortunately, school is a highly organized activity that occurs on a near daily basis. Regular routines like this, even if they conflict with the program, are not major sources of disruption. Unless the school is posing unusual problems for your child, no changes are needed. See Chapter 12 for guidelines in how to select a school that will complement what you are doing at home.

What do I do about my child's stimming when I'm driving the car?

In situations where you have no control, the basic principle is to ignore the behavior. If you say something such as,

"Stop that," you have no way to enforce it. That sends the message that you have no ability to control your child. Although it may not be ideal, ignoring the behavior is the preferable way to go. Minimizing time in the car is also helpful.

My child constantly asks for music in the car. What should I do?

If the music is calming, you can play it. However, if your child issues commands for you to constantly change the music, simply say, "Not now." The child may object in the beginning, but if you show consistency, more appropriate and less demanding behavior will follow.

12

Expanding the Partnership

The lives of all children extend beyond the home. They go to school, they participate in community activities, they have music lessons—to name just a few. The right types of services and activities can enrich a child's life and foster growth.

A potential complication for children on the spectrum, however, is that they can wind up having too many services. Although it's easy to understand why this happens, it's important to recognize that more is not necessarily better. The potential disadvantages of multiple services include

- hours of one-to-one interaction that can overwhelm the child's resources;

- overstimulation that leads the child to be too fatigued to use the input effectively; and

- contradictory approaches which add confusion to the child's world.

Your goal is to implement the services that offer the greatest potential benefit. Here are some guidelines to help you do that.

School

Schools are an invaluable resource. We are not talking here about the content of instruction, for that involves issues beyond the scope of this book. What we are talking about is the basic setup, where long periods of predictable routines are steadily present. These offer zones of security for the children. Equally important, schools provide hours of relief to parents. Those hours are essential in allowing parents to get some distance from the intense work of raising a child on the spectrum and to gain time to handle the essentials of life.

Still, schools generally follow principles that are quite different from those of this program. That inevitably leads parents to ask, "Will my child be confused by the lack of consistency?"

Consistency is, obviously, the ideal. The good news, though, is that consistency between the home and the school is not essential. Just as children can differentiate among the different contexts at home, they can differentiate between home and other settings. As long as home life is running smoothly, they can tolerate the differences at school. It is a bit like learning to be bilingual. The children know that one set of rules applies at home and one set of rules applies at school.

Fortunately, with children six years of age and younger, the improved behavior at home often transfers to other settings. Parents tell us that school personnel are delighted by the children's improved behavior in the classroom. This welcome byproduct is not surprising. It is one of the positive effects of all the work you have been doing.

On occasion, schools are able to implement some aspects of the program. For example, one school had struggled with a particular child for several years. He was extraordinarily difficult to manage and regularly disrupted the class. The staff was desperate for help. When they heard that the child was starting a new program at home, they asked if they could do the program at school. It worked extremely well, and the child made rapid progress.

This, however, is the exception rather than the rule. Institutional change generally requires a great deal of time and effort. Administrators are pleased when they can achieve significant change within five years. This type of change is wonderful for the generation that follows, but it does not serve your child who will have long left the class where you hoped to achieve the modifications.

Even when schools are interested, they are limited by a range of constraints that prevent effective implementation of the program. For example, in some states teachers are not allowed to touch students or they are greatly restricted in how they can do this. In one region where we have worked, adults can touch a child only if the child has engaged in three consecutive aggressive behaviors. Rules of this sort make it impossible to carry out simple actions such as holding the child's hands—a procedure that is critical to achieving more focused interaction.

How to Select a Good Classroom Environment

In recent years, parents have begun to have greater influence over the school their child attends. If you have a choice of schools, select one where you see classrooms that function in a calm, smooth way. On the surface, you might describe them as "boring."

In using this term, we do not mean to imply that nothing is going on. The children and adults should be engaged in focused activities. Often it's not given the credit it merits, but considerable talent is needed for a teacher to create a classroom that runs so easily that it seems as though nothing unusual is happening. This is particularly the case when the class is composed of children with significant developmental disabilities where temper tantrums, meltdowns, and aggressive actions can so easily happen.

When teachers are able to maintain a social setting where calmness prevails, that is an outstanding achievement. That type of calm control—in a multi-person social setting—serves in a variety of ways to enhance children's development. It provides them with a sense of ease and relaxation when they are with other people.

You can also play a significant role in creating the Individualized Education Plan (IEP) and the services it lists for your child. Even though it is tempting, your major goal should not be to get as many therapy hours as possible. If at all possible, you should aim to observe your child in the therapy sessions that are offered. That gives you the opportunity to observe the interaction between your child and the therapist.

What you should look for is whether your child is responding effectively or whether your child is engaging in a variety of avoidance behaviors. No child needs additional practice in avoiding interaction; that serves only to reinforce the social problems. It may well be that as your child improves, you will want to reinstate some therapy that has not been effective in the past. The key is to minimize exposure to therapies where your child is demonstrating a high level of resistance and avoidance.

If you are relatively new to the school scene, it's natural to feel somewhat intimidated by the process. Other parents can provide valuable guidance. In addition, many communities have parent advocates who are available to work with you in establishing the best educational curriculum for your child. For more information, you may find it helpful to go to http://www.ed-center.com/special_education_advocate.

Services Outside the School

In evaluating services outside the school, your goal is to become an educated, discerning consumer. Parents often feel pressure to turn matters over to the professionals and let them do their job. Try not to give in to this pressure and try not to underestimate your own abilities. Even though there will be many aspects of your child's medical and educational treatment that are too complex to fully understand, you can master the fundamentals.

Consider one example. Speech and language therapies are among the first services offered to children on the spectrum since most have severely limited skills in spoken language. Parents are often delighted since it seems to be precisely what their child needs.

However, when behavioral control is not in place and when some fundamental prerequisites of language are not in place, the introduction of speech therapy can be a case of "too much, too fast." This is why, after years of therapy, a high percentage of the children remain with little or no functional speech.

At the same time, the pressure to produce spoken language generates high levels of resistance that can exacerbate the children's difficulties. It is a lose-lose situation. An educated and observant parent is the best protection against this unfortunate course of action getting underway.

Below are some guidelines that can help you make informed decisions about your child's services.

GUIDELINE 1: SETTING A TIME FRAME

If a program does not yield noticeable results within three months, you should consider stopping that service, or at least putting it on hold for several months.

GUIDELINE 2: ENSURING HOME PRACTICE

The content of most services involves skills that need frequent practice. This includes the behaviors taught in speech and language therapy, occupational therapy, physical therapy, and cognitive therapy. For example, if occupational therapy is limited to one or even two periods a week, the likelihood of the skills being incorporated into the child's daily life is very low, at best.

One of the best ways to maximize results is to carry out daily five to ten minute exercises with your child. To do this, ask the therapist to provide a list of activities that complement what is being done in the therapist's office and are easy to implement at home.

This view is not shared by all therapists, so if you wish to implement this guideline, it is important to find a therapist who sees the value of practicing the skills at home.

GUIDELINE 3: OBSERVING THE SESSIONS

Regularly observe your child's therapy sessions. If benefits are to be gained from the intervention, you should see that the child is responsive to the therapist's demands. If that is not the case, discuss this with the therapist. If nothing can be done to change matters, consider consulting another specialist in the area or putting the therapy on hold until the child's behavior has improved.

Other parents are a great source of information and guidance. Ask around to find out which therapists in your community are highly recommended by other parents. The sign of a good teacher, tutor, or coach is one whose former students have excelled.

GUIDELINE 4: ANALYZE THE CONSISTENCY OF THE VARIOUS THERAPIES

Examine the content in the range of therapies that your child is receiving and see if contradictions exist. For example, if your child is in the early stages of our program where language input is kept to a minimum, you should observe to see how your child's therapists use language.

You may well find that the therapist (regardless of discipline) speaks to the child primarily in questions and uses a level of language that is much too complex for the child to understand. Should this be the case, you would need to determine if (a) the therapist is open to modifying the language, (b) a new therapist is preferable, or (c) the therapy should be put off for a period.

GUIDELINE 5: FOCUSING ON THE ACTIVITY NOT THE PERSONALITY

Do not focus on whether your child likes the therapist. Often the children prefer therapists who will do what they want rather than what they need. That's no surprise. But it is a factor that undermines the therapeutic goals. What you should seek is a therapist who, without being harsh or negative, effectively gets your child to progress on key skills.

GUIDELINE 6: ADDING NEW PROGRAMS GRADUALLY

If your child is adjusting to a change of some kind—it may be that you are trying a new diet, or a new medicine, or a new babysitter—consider holding off on any new therapies until an equilibrium has been reached. It's best to allow your child to reach a steady state before introducing a significant new set of demands.

The good news is that you may find that when the steady state is reached, a particular therapy is no longer needed.

One two-year-old boy, for example, was referred to us on the grounds that he had language and communication delays. As often occurs in situations of this sort, he also had a number of behavioral issues, including resistance to any demands imposed by an adult and steady avoidance of interaction with adults. Within three months of starting the program, the resistance was markedly lessened. With that improvement, he became far more interested in and attentive to adults. The end result was that, as with a neurotypical child, his language skyrocketed and language therapy was not needed.

Nutrition

Problems with diet and nutrition are common in children on the spectrum and many benefit from consultation with a nutritionist. The types of problems that often need to be addressed are

- low food intake—when an insufficient number of calories is consumed

- high food intake—with an excess of "empty" calories and an abundance of processed foods

- food allergies that may range from mild (occasional itching and rings under the eyes) to severe (vomiting, diarrhea, skin rashes, and abdominal pain)

- inadequate fiber and fluid intake, leading to chronic constipation

- mild to severe nutrient deficiencies (for example, particular vitamins or minerals may be deficient)

- difficulty adhering to a specific diet prescribed by a physician

The principles we outlined in Part 2 are useful in handling many of these problems. The following guidelines are also helpful:

GUIDELINE 7: SELECTING NUTRIENT-RICH FOOD

A healthy diet is essential for children on the spectrum to reach their full potential in behavior and cognition. The goal is not just for a functional diet but an optimal one. Evidence is growing that many children with ASD have subtle differences in metabolism, making them more vulnerable to nutrient deficiencies.

This means that children on the spectrum should avoid unhealthy, processed foods. The best course of action is to remove these foods from the home. Otherwise the children will continue to seek them.

GUIDELINE 8: OFFERING HEALTHY BUT APPEALING FOODS

Make a list of all the healthy foods that your child has ever eaten. Your goal is to offer healthy foods that have some appeal to the child so that you can avoid a struggle during mealtime. In the beginning there may only be a small number of foods that the child will accept. Over time, you can expand the child's diet by introducing small amounts of new foods gradually. Select new foods carefully, so that they are similar to ones that the child already accepts. For example, if the only fruit your child likes is apples, begin to think of how to introduce a small slice of pear at a meal. Then introduce two slices of pear the next day, and so on. With consistency and attention, most children can learn to accept a wider variety of healthy foods over time.

GUIDELINE 9: PLANNING MEALTIME

As indicated in Chapter 9, there should be three meals a day. If your child wishes, there can also be two snacks. Plan in advance so that you are prepared with healthy, appealing foods to offer. In the beginning all meals and snacks should be healthy and appealing to the child, but you will be the one selecting the foods. In general, do not ask your child what food he or she wants. This can lead to unnecessary difficulties (e.g., some children have difficulty making choices, others will always choose the same food, and so on). Your goal should be to offer foods the child likes, but not ones he or she selects.

As we described in Chapter 9, limit the length of the meal to about 20 minutes. The child must sit at a table that is of an appropriate size so that his or her feet touch the ground. This may require that you purchase a small table and chair.

In the beginning you need to be near the child in order to handle any issues that arise. The child should eat alone with you nearby. Other children and family members should eat at another time. In addition, the atmosphere should be quiet with no TV or other devices on. Conversation should be minimal.

Any unproductive behaviors should be handled using the techniques described in Chapters 6 and 7. For children who eat too quickly, cut the food into small bite-size portions and put only one piece at a time on the plate. When that piece has been chewed and swallowed, put out another piece and continue in this manner.

A Special Set of Activities—the Ones Your Child Loves

In most conventional therapies it's not relevant as to whether or not the child likes the therapy. There is an important exception to this rule. When you identify activities that your child truly enjoys—such as swimming, music, horseback riding, or others—the activity should become a regular part of the child's life.

Sometimes these interests flourish and the child shows real expertise in a particular area. For example, some children show extraordinary genius-quality skills in music, art, or math.

Whether your child's interests reflect extraordinary talent or just simple pleasure, these interests should be nurtured since they bring the child so much joy. It's up to you to determine the extent to which you do this and at what pace. For example, you may want to have a piano at home for the child to play as he or she chooses. As the child grows, you may decide to hire a piano instructor who can help the child reach new levels of skill. The goal is to make a place in your child's life for constructive activities that bring him or her pleasure.

· ·

FREQUENTLY ASKED QUESTIONS:

My daughter loves pouring water and it can keep her occupied for hours. Should I consider that an "appealing activity" and allow her to indulge in it?

Pouring water is a form of stimming. It is a type of activity that does not lead to any new learning. It is not harmful if limited to short periods of time (five or ten minutes), but longer periods should not be allowed. Simple, repetitive activities that enable the child to tune out from the world for long periods are not the ones that should be encouraged. They should be handled according to the techniques described in Part 2.

The activities to be encouraged are those that involve the learning of skills that

- contain an inherent organization and
- require sustained activity for them to be achieved.

These include playing a musical instrument, athletics, art, and others.

My daughter eats only Cheerios and French fries. How can I extend her diet?

It can be useful to slowly introduce tiny amounts of new foods in the following way. Begin with foods that your child is likely to accept (e.g., if she accepts potatoes, she might accept sweet potatoes). At the outset of the meal when she is likely to be most hungry, put one tiny piece of sweet potato on a plate. Do not show your daughter any other food. When she has eaten it, bring the French fries close and continue on with the usual meal. On following days, increase to two, then three pieces of sweet potato. Through this approach, her diet will be likely to expand in a gradual and consistent manner.

Preview to the Next Step

Teaching Language and Reading

With a spectacular bond in place, your child is ready for a true teacher-student partnership. This means you can now focus on significant cognitive skills that you want your child to master. For most parents, language tops the list. The Spectacular Bond program provides two paths for teaching language to children ages two years and over.

- **ASD Language,** which teaches spoken language

- **ASD Reading,** which teaches written language (reading and writing)

This dual route, which is unique to the Spectacular Bond program, allows children to advance in language through either one or both systems. Each program is extensive and includes a wealth of content—from beginner to advanced levels. Detailed information is available at www.asdlanguage.com and www.asdreading.com.

Below is a brief overview of the programs.

ASD Language and ASD Reading

Language represents a vast range of skills. Unfortunately, there has been a lack of consensus among professionals about which skills to teach children on the spectrum. By default, the dominant approach has been to teach children to produce short, one- or two-word responses, usually to a variety of unrelated questions such as "What color is that?" "Who is that?" or "What shape is that?"

Effective language requires far more. Imagine trying to have a real conversation when all you can say are single words and a few scripted phrases. Both **ASD Language** and **ASD Reading** are designed to achieve the breadth of skills needed for true communication. As reflected in a mother's comments below, the skills that the children master often exceed what parents had thought was possible.

> Do you remember what Sophie was like a year ago? She spoke in strings of disconnected phrases that we couldn't understand. She never spoke in sentences unless she was scripting, and even then nothing she said made sense.
>
> This morning she said something totally different! She told me about a real experience that happened on a trip we took a few weeks ago. This is how the conversation went:
>
>> Sophie: Remember when we saw that bird, that seagull, eating a fish?
>>
>> Mother: A seagull eating a fish?
>>
>> Sophie: Yes, when we were going to the water park.
>>
>> Mother: Oh yes, I remember that.
>>
>> Sophie: It was right before we went over the bridge. We went over the bridge and then we went to the water park.
>
> Until now, she would never talk about a past experience without a lot of prompting and coaching.

> This was spontaneous and accurate! It is truly amazing the progress she has made.

What is equally exciting is that comparable achievements are possible for children who do not speak—children who are considered "nonverbal." For these children, reading and writing offer an alternate route to language. Not only does the world of written language offer all the components of a full language system, but it also has the added advantage of presenting language via the visual system. As a result, it capitalizes on the inherent strengths in visual processing present in many of the children. That makes it a priceless tool for children on the spectrum whose speech is severely compromised.

ASD Reading is the program that teaches reading and writing to children with ASD. It is effective for children who have spoken language and are ready to expand their language and cognitive skills. It is also effective for children who do not yet speak.

Many parents and professionals are surprised to hear that the children can learn to read before they learn to speak. We have seen this again and again in our work, and there are a growing number of individuals with ASD who have written about their experience learning to read and write before they could speak. A research study at Columbia University using a reading curriculum developed by Dr. Blank demonstrated that nonverbal children with autistic disorder were able to acquire skills in reading and writing (go to www.spectacularbond.com for more information).

ASD Reading begins by teaching children to read, write, and understand simple words, phrases, and sentences. Within a few months, children advance to complex sentences linked by a theme, such as the following:

Animals have babies, and their babies need many things. They need food to eat, water to drink, and good places to stay. Those are some of the things they need.

Children who do not speak begin with **ASD Reading**. Many of them can learn to speak at a later time when their oral-motor skills advance.

In summary, **ASD Language** is the program to start with for children on the spectrum who can already speak. Many continue on to **ASD Reading** as well since reading and writing are the next steps in education for all children. For those children who do not speak, **ASD Reading** is the program to start with. Many of these children can go on to learn spoken language as well. Both programs can be implemented by a parent, teacher, therapist, or other dedicated adult.

Epilogue

March 28, 2012

It's Diane's twelfth birthday. I am walking down the main hallway of her school. As I approach Diane's locker, I see that it has been beautifully decorated with pictures and ribbons. Dozens of thoughtful messages from her classmates are written across a colorful banner.

I see Diane walking toward me, beaming. "Look, mom!" she says, "My friends decorated my locker for my birthday!" My eyes well up with tears.

When Diane was in preschool, I doubted that she would ever be able to speak, read, write, form friendships, or have any chance of making it on her own. I could not have imagined that she would have the full life that she has now.

I see many parents of young children on the spectrum facing those same fears. For those parents, my message is one of hope. I have seen what Diane has accomplished. Her life is filled with interests, hobbies, friendships, and love. She can handle most everything in life that comes at her. Her future looks vastly different than what I imagined years ago.

Best of all, we have a close mother-daughter relationship. She confides in me about her latest crush, and I guide her through the ups and downs of the pre-teen years. We are two partners who have built an amazing relationship despite the tremendous obstacles that stood in our way. None of this would have been possible if we had allowed her to stay in the disorganized, isolated world of autism that trapped her for the first years of her life.

Ours is a bond that is truly spectacular.

Susan Deland

Further Reading

Chapter 2. The World Through the Child's Eyes

pg 37: Grandin, T., & Scariano, M. (1986) *Emergence: Labeled Autistic*. Novato, CA: Arena Press, p.18.

pg 38: Personal Perspectives on Autism

Barron, J. and Barron, S. (2002) *There's a Boy in Here*. Future Horizons: Arlington, TX.
A story told by a mother and son about the son's early years with autism.

Blackman, L. (2009) *Lucy's Story: Autism and Other Adventures*. Jessica Kingsley Publishers: London.
A woman with autism describes her quest as a child to understand what was said around her.

Brosen, S. K. (2006) *Do You Understand Me?* Jessica Kingsley Publishers: London.
An eleven-year-old girl's account of her day-to-day life with autism and its challenges.

Cowhey, S.P. (2005) *Going Through The Motions: Coping With Autism*. Publish America: Frederick, MD.
A woman's account of her challenges with autism.

Grandin, T. (2008) *The Way I See It: A Personal Look at Autism and Asperger's*. Future Horizons: Arlington, TX.
A book by the acclaimed animal scientist, with her personal reflections on autism and the challenges she faced as a child.

Hammerschmidt, E. (2008) *Born on the Wrong Planet.* Autism Asperger's Publishing Company: Overland Park, KS.

An American woman with autism writes about the inner workings of her mind.

Mukhopadhyay, T.R. (2011) *How Can I Talk If My Lips Don't Move?: Inside My Autistic Mind.* Arcade Publishing: New York, NY.

A young Indian man's account, in narrative and prose poems, about how his autistic mind thinks, sees, and reacts to the world.

Nazeer, K. (2006) *Send in the Idiots: Stories from the Other Side of Autism.* Bloomsbury: London.

A man describes the difficult early lives of himself and four classmates at a former school for children with autism in New York City in the early 1980s.

Sellin, B. and Bell, A. (1996) *I Don't Want to Be Inside Me Anymore: Messages from an Autistic Mind.* Basic Books: New York.

A German man gives a firsthand account of his life with autism.

Williams, D. (1998) *Autism and Sensing: The Unlost Instinct.* Jessica Kingsley Publishers: London.

An Australian woman with autism explains how the senses of a person with autism work, suggesting that they are "stuck" at an early developmental stage common to everyone.

pg 38: Grandin, T. (1995) *Thinking in Pictures: and Other Reports from My Life with Autism.* New York, NY: Vintage. p. 62.

pg 38: Grandin, T. "An Inside View of Autism." Indiana Institute of Disability and Community. 13 March 2013. http://www.iidc.indiana.edu/index.php?pageid=595

pg 38: Stehli, A. (1991) *The Sound of a Miracle: A Child's Triumph Over Autism.* New York, NY: Doubleday. p. 187.

pg 38: Williams, D. (1992) *Nobody Nowhere: The Extraordinary Autobiography of an Autistic*. New York: Time Books. p. 8.

pg 39: Williams, D. (1994) *Somebody Somewhere: Breaking Free from the World of Autism*. New York: Time Books. p. 32.

pg 39: Grandin, T. & Scariano, M. (1986) *Emergence: Labeled Autistic*. Novato, CA: Arena Press. p. 19.

pg 39: Markram, H., Rinaldi, T., & Markram, K. (2007) "The Intense World Syndrome—an alternative hypothesis for autism." *Frontiers in Neuroscience*. 1(1): 77–96.

pg 46: Kranowitz, C.S. (2005) *The Out-of-Sync Child: Recognizing and Coping with Sensory Processing Disorder*. New York, NY: Skylight Press.

Chapter 3. The Parent's Search for the "Key"

pg 52: Kanner, L. (1943) "Autistic Disturbances of Affective Contact." *The Nervous Child Journal 2*. p. 41.

pg 57: Wallace, K.S. & Rogers, S. J. (2010) "Intervening in infancy: implications for autism spectrum disorders." *Journal of Child Psychology and Psychiatry*. 51(12):1300–1320.

Chapter 4. New Possibilities: Tapping into Neuroscience

pg 63: Herbert, M. (2012) *The Autism Revolution: Whole-Body Strategies for Making Life All It Can Be*. Random House: New York. p. 24.

pg 65: Hyde, K.L., *et al.* (2009) "The Effects of Musical Training on Structural Brain Development: A Longitudinal Study." *The Neurosciences and Music III: Disorders and Plasticity: Annals of the New York Academy of Sciences*. 1169:182–186.

pg 65: Gaser, C. & Schlaug, G. (2003) "Brain Structures Differ between Musicians and Non-Musicians." *Journal of Neuroscience.* 23(27): 9240–9245.

pg 65: Pascual-Leone, A. & Torres, F. (1993) "Plasticity of the sensorimotor cortex representation of the reading finger in Braille readers." *Brain.* 116(Pt1):39–52.

pg 65: Van Boven, R.W. *et al.* (2000) "Tactile spatial resolution in blind Braille readers." *Neurology.* 54:2230–2236.

pg 65: Maguire, E.A. *et al.* (2000) Navigation-related structural change in the hippocampi of taxi drivers. *Proceedings of the National Academy of Sciences.* 97(8):4398–4403.

pg 65: Woollett, K. & Maguire, E.A. (2011) Acquiring "the Knowledge" of London's Layout Drives Structural Brain Changes. *Current Biology.* 21(24):2109–2114.

pg 66: Dawson, G. *et al.* (2012) "Early behavioral intervention is associated with normalized brain activity in young children with autism." *Journal of the American Academy of Child and Adolescent Psychiatry.* 51(11):1150–1159.

pg 68: Kedar, I. (2012) *Ido in Autismland: Climbing Out of Autism's Silent Prison.* San Bernadino, CA: Ido Kedar. p. 42.

pg 69: Herbert, M. (2012) *The Autism Revolution: Whole-Body Strategies for Making Life All It Can Be.* Random House: New York. p. 11.

pg 71: Adolphs R. (2003) "Cognitive neuroscience of human social behaviour." *Nature Reviews Neuroscience.* 4(3):165–178.

pg 71: Fossati P. (2012) "Neural correlates of emotion processing: from emotional to social brain." *European Neuropsychopharmacology.* 22(Suppl 3):S487–491.

Chapter 6. Building Self-Control

pg 107: Fleischmann, A. (2012) *Carly's Voice*, New York, NY: Touchstone. p. 376.

Chapter 7. Managing Meltdowns

pg 139: Grandin, T., & Scariano, M. (1986) *Emergence: Labeled Autistic*. Novato, CA: Arena Press. p. 28.

Books of Related Interest:

Managing Meltdowns: Using the S.C.A.R.E.D. Calming Technique with Children and Adults with Autism. By Deborah Lipsky and Will Richards (2009) Jessica Kingsley Publishers. Philadelphia.

From Anxiety to Meltdown: How Individuals on the Autism Spectrum Deal with Anxiety, Experience Meltdowns, Manifest Tantrums, and How You Can Intervene Effectively. By Deborah Lipsky (2011) Jessica Kingsley Publishers. Philadelphia.

Managing the Cycle of Meltdowns for Students with Autism Spectrum Disorder. By Geoffrey T. Colvin and Martin R. Sheehan (2012) Corwin A Sage Company. Thousand Oaks, CA.

Asperger Syndrome and Difficult Moments: Practical Solutions for Tantrums, Rage and Meltdowns. By Brenda Smith Myles and Jack Southwick (2005) Autism Asperger Publishing Co. Shawnee Mission, Kansas.

Chapter 8. Sitting Quietly

pg 153: Lutz, A. *et al.* "Long-term meditators self-induce high-amplitude gamma synchrony during mental practice." *Proceedings of the National Academy of Sciences.* 2004; 101(46): 16369–73.

pg 153: Lutz, A. *et al.* "Mental training enhances attentional stability: neural and behavioral evidence." *Journal of Neuroscience.* 2009; 29(42): 13418–27.

Websites of Related Interest

http://www.autismkey.com/meditation-and-autism/

http://dailyheal.com/meditation-news/autism-adhd-and-meditation/

http://autism.healingthresholds.com/therapy/meditation

Chapter 10. Moving On

pg 192: Kedar, I. (2012) *Ido in Autismland: Climbing Out of Autism's Silent Prison.* San Bernadino, CA: Ido Kedar. p. 78.

Chapter 12. Expanding the Partnership

pg 217: Herbert, M. (2012) *The Autism Revolution: Whole-Body Strategies for Making Life All It Can Be.* Random House: New York.

Preview to the Next Step: Teaching Your Child to Speak, Read, and Write

pg 223: Accounts of individuals with ASD who have learned written language before spoken language:

Eastham, M. Grice, A. (1992) *Silent Words: A Biography.* Ottawa: Oliver-Pate.

Fleischmann, A. (2012) *Carly's Voice,* New York, NY: Touchstone.

Kedar, I. (2012) *Ido in Autismland: Climbing Out of Autism's Silent Prison.* San Bernadino, CA: Ido Kedar.

Mukhopadhyay, T.R. & Wing, L. (2000) *Beyond the Silence: My Life, the World and Autism.* Iola, KS: Central.

Index

W

T

V

Made in the USA
Columbia, SC
17 October 2017